WHEN DREAMS TAKE FLIGHT

WHEN DREAMS TAKE
FLIGHT

Lessons to Help You SOAR Through Life

DON SMITH

nEXT CEnTURY
PUBLISHING

When Dreams Take Flight – Lessons to Help You Soar Through Life

Published by Next Century Publishing
www.NextCenturyPublishing.com
Las Vegas, NV

ISBN: 978-1-62903-824-7

Library of Congress Control Number: 2015900745

www.whendreamstakeflight.net

Printed in the United States of America

I dedicate this book to my wife Ellen and my daughter Yolanda. I would also like to dedicate it to my four granddaughters, Rhonda, Natalie, Laura, and Leisha; and to my three great grandchildren, Gabriel, Eva, and Luke.

WHEN DREAMS TAKE
FLIGHT

Table of Contents

Prologue

I tossed and turned, trying to get comfortable in my modest bed. It was another hot summer evening, and there was no breeze to bring relief from the stifling heat. Trying to get settled in hope of succumbing to sleep, I listened to the sounds of the evening—the poignant overtures of the classical music station on the radio contrasted with my sister's ebullient chattering about the happenings at school that day. I found myself smiling at the familiar sounds, but sleep continued to elude me.

Only one thing was on my mind. It was the month before my thirteenth birthday on the fourteenth of July. I didn't know why I was so excited about it. The previous four or five birthdays had been just ordinary days. My life had been anything but easy up until this point in my life. I felt anxiety creep up inside me as I thought about my rather insecure existence; we moved frequently and never seemed to have enough money to go around. I had no reason to anticipate that my birthday would be a special day at all. However, being an optimist, I was imagining a grand occasion.

I was a dreamer. Sometimes I would lie in the field near our home, daydreaming and watching the airplanes that soared above me, far beyond the struggles that I so desperately wanted to overcome.

Now, I stretched myself out on my small bed, imagining what it would be like to be that high above the clouds—it seemed an impossible feat to my young mind, but I felt a longing that I did not quite understand.

As moonlight ushered in the night and the crickets began their song, I closed my eyes and imagined myself up in the clouds, arms outstretched, rising and falling with the winds. My trifling uncertainties became distant as I climbed higher and higher, soaring high above the cares and trials of the earth below.

Life Lesson #1

Live Your Life with DETERMINATION

"The difference between the impossible and the possible
lies in a man's determination."

—Tommy Lasorda

I had to be a pilot. Not just any professional pilot, but the best in the world.

One late afternoon as the sun burned high in the western sky, my flight instructor, Mr. Jimenez, and I had been practicing touch-and-go landings for what seemed like an eternity. All I was expecting that day was my few hours of weekly flight time that my menial work at the airport terminal would bargain. We were flying an old Fleet, an open cockpit biplane with a radial engine. After a full stop landing, Mr. Jimenez told me to taxi back to the end of the runway. When we were on the run-up apron, he got out of the airplane and asked me if I thought I could take off and fly the airplane by myself. He thought I could do it, but he just wanted to know if I felt the same way. I didn't hesitate to say yes. He walked away from the airplane and gave me a salute.

All of a sudden, it hit me! I was going to fly "solo." My heart pounded inside my chest.

Can I really do it? All of the hours I had spent practicing with Mr. Jimenez and visualizing the cockpit controls while completing various mundane tasks came down to this one moment. This was really happening!

My fears and doubts slowly vanished as I started reviewing the procedures I had been using for the last hour or so. I lined up the airplane on the runway, took one last glance at Mr. Jimenez, and added power. I was a little late using right rudder to compensate for engine torque, so the airplane started to veer to the left, which made me remember to use right rudder. After "S"ing on either side of the runway centerline a couple of times, I finally settled down and kept it rolling on a straight line.

Before I knew it, I was airborne! What a feeling. But the euphoria was short-lived.

The airplane leaped into the air a lot sooner than what I was accustomed to without the weight of my instructor. I should have been expecting it, but in the middle of my anxiety, all I could think was that something went drastically wrong. I lost my confidence. All I wanted to do was get that "beast" on the ground, and even though I had just spent hours practicing just that, I didn't think I was capable of doing it.

As I was maneuvering the airplane around the pattern, I promised myself that, if by some miracle, I could get safely on the ground, I would never ever fly again. I just kept doing everything mechanically, the way I had been doing it the previous eight to ten times around the pattern. I turned to base leg, then to final. I reduced power, and I aimed for the end of the runway. The ground was coming at me! I mechanically pulled the control stick back, closing the throttle; suddenly, I heard the swish of the landing gear wheels turning. I had never made a landing as smoothly as that one! Mr. Jimenez was waiting midfield. As I turned off the grass strip, he came running to the airplane.

"That was beautiful!" he said as he shook my hand. "Take it up again."

I forgot all about the promise I had made to myself just a few minutes earlier. I knew I could do it! I taxied back to the end of the runway, lined up with the runway centerline, and added power, remembering to use right rudder. Then I made what I thought was a perfect takeoff.

This second time in the air I thoroughly enjoyed the scenery. I even extended the legs around the pattern. I was really living! I thought about all of the sacrifices I had made to get to this point and how proud my mother would be of me. Every instance of determination in the face of adversity had brought me to this moment of triumph.

I finally began to make my approach, and I thought I was doing everything the way I had done it before. However, my second landing was anything but beautiful. I bounced twice and finally came to a stop, but not very gracefully. That's overconfidence for you, I suppose. But I didn't care because I knew I could do it. I was the happiest guy on earth. I had flown an airplane by myself, and now I knew I was unstoppable. Mr. Jimenez was shaking his head as he approached the airplane, but he had a smile on his face.

My face mirrored his smile, knowing what that solo flight had meant to me. More than ever, I wanted to do whatever it took to reach my goal of being the best professional pilot the world had ever seen. I knew it wouldn't be easy. But I had learned throughout my short life that nothing that is worthwhile in this life comes easily. It comes with dogged determination to do whatever it takes, in spite of any and every obstacle you face. When you have an unyielding determination driving you forward, you will most certainly achieve your goals. *Live your life with determination!*

Questions

1. During the take-off roll, the author had to correct his path with the left and right rudders to compensate for engine torque. He was pleased that he remembered how to do it. Why are course corrections sometimes necessary to keep going on the right path in life?

2. The author took off unexpectedly because of the difference in the weight of the plane without his instructor. He spent the entirety of his first solo flight in so much anxiety that he didn't even get to enjoy being up in the air! Have you ever experienced a similar situation where anxiety kept you from enjoying the pleasures of life? Share your experience.

3. The author, after being encouraged by his instructor to get back out there, took the airplane back up into the sky. This time, he was able to enjoy the sights all around him and think about everything that had gotten him to that day. What goals are you determined to achieve in your life? Can you imagine what it would be like to finally achieve them and "soar," much like the author did in a literal sense, over your circumstances?

Life Lesson #2

Live Your Life with HOPE

*"Man can live about forty days without food,
about three days without water, about eight minutes without air ... but only
for one second without hope."*

—Hal Lindsey

Even as I soared above the clouds, the memory of a desperate childhood still hung in the air like a thick fog grounding the plane of my life. I thought back to my early years and the devastation we experienced after my stepfather left us. We were forced to sell all of our belongings and move in with a friend of my mother's just to survive. I thought that we had hit rock bottom. Life could not possibly get any worse.

I was wrong.

Although the Villada family was gracious enough to give us a temporary home, we still had no money, and Luz Maria barely made enough to feed herself and her small family. How I wished I could take care of my mother. I knew she would try to find a job, but she didn't have any training, and it was unthinkable for her to get involved in manual labor due to our social status. So my mother, my sister, and I would leave early in the morning before they had breakfast to try to find a way to make money. We would separate and wish each other luck.

As one can imagine, my choices of things to do to earn money were very limited at my tender age of twelve. I spent most of the time walking the streets and dreaming about fame and fortune, knowing deep within me that this condition had to be temporary and that someday we would be out of it. I didn't know how I sustained that hope through the desolation of our circumstances, but I knew I had to have that belief and faith to keep me going. Otherwise, I would have succumbed to despair. After a day of futilely searching for a job, I would return to Luz Maria's house to see how my mother and sister had fared. Sometimes my mother would bring some food. We never knew how she got it, but she would give it to Estercita, Luz Maria's mother, to show that we were able to contribute.

This routine went on for several weeks. I started to get used to one meal a day, but my body did not deal with the change easily. It would begin with a headache. Then all the right side of my vision would become green, causing severe nausea. When this happened I had to sit, put my head in my hands, and let it pass. If I was out looking for a job, I had to sit on the sidewalk, sometimes for a couple of hours, before I could get going again. This was just another obstacle keeping me from finding work.

Of course, school was out of the question under those conditions. I felt that my primary responsibility was to work and help my mother and sister survive. There were no welfare programs or any other kind of help for those in need. Even if these kinds of programs had been available, our family would have been too proud to accept the assistance. The choices were work, steal, beg, or starve. We were too afraid to steal, too proud to beg, and we couldn't find a job, so we went without food. Right or wrong, it was our nature to make these decisions in that way.

The one positive activity I was able to keep throughout this ordeal was reading, which gave me great joy. One of the first things I would do when I went out each day was look for magazines that people had thrown away. Occasionally I found my favorite, the Spanish translation of the *Reader's Digest*, and I would read it from cover to cover. That filled a lot of the otherwise empty and hungry hours. It was my window to what the world was like outside of that miserable existence. It was a way to keep my optimism, reminding me that this was a temporary situation and enabling me to go on. It was a small beacon of hope that, someday, things might change for the better.

The days turned into weeks, and the weeks into months. Except for the daily dose of optimism and love we received from my mother, the situation got bleaker every day. It finally became obvious that we couldn't remain in Luz Maria's house. We didn't like the idea of being a burden. So·one day, my mother was able to scrape together a few pesos and told Luz Maria that she had gotten a job, and we were moving to an apartment. Of course, my mother hadn't gotten a job, but she thought it would ease Luz Maria's mind. We moved our few remaining belongings to a furnished rooming house. It only had one bed, so my mother and sister slept on it, while I slept on newspapers on the floor. We continued our routine of going out to look for a job with no success.

I returned to our room around eight o'clock one night, weak with hunger. My sister was there, hungry as well, having not eaten all day. We were sure that my mother would bring something to eat, as she always had since we moved to the room. She arrived around ten o'clock, empty-handed. That was probably one of the few times we saw her without her usual smile. We looked at each other and realized that we had to try to sleep, even with our stomachs aching from hunger. It was the first time we hadn't eaten at least one meal during the day. I'll always remember that night: the hunger, the pain, and the hopelessness of the situation.

A strange thing happened around midnight when I finally convinced myself that we were not going to eat anything that night—as well as probably the next day. I lost my hunger. It was as if I had just flipped a switch. This ability really helped me in the following three years, as our situation didn't improve and even got worse at times. There were stretches when we didn't eat for two or three days at a time.

We had to move from the rooming house when we were unable to pay rent. However, since our appearance was still that of a respectable middle-class family, the landlady allowed us to move to another room. She didn't even worry about the fact that my mother didn't have the money for the first week's rent. No matter how low we got, in our minds we were broke, not poor. We never let anyone know what we were going through. We were too proud and kept telling ourselves, "Surely tomorrow will be better."

While my mother was searching for a job, she met the chief of Mexico City International Airport, Commander Jose Cora. She asked him if he thought he could give me a job at the airport, and he told her to send me to see him the following week.

I really didn't want to go; it was too far, and I was afraid I would go all the way to the airport just to be told no. I thought it would be more productive to look around closer to where we were living, especially since I didn't even have money for the bus most of the time. But my mother insisted I go to see Commander Cora. I was hesitant, but I had to make her proud.

I finally made the trip to the airport. I remember how insignificant I felt when I walked into the air terminal. It was about one-tenth the size of today's terminals and rather archaic, but to me it seemed like the most beautiful structure I had ever seen. I could see huge airplanes (DC-3s) parked outside. I had never seen an airplane on the ground—only in the air where they looked so small. I had wondered what manner of supermen could be flying in those shiny airplanes. The whole idea of people flying seemed like a frightful and impossible achievement. But here they were. I actually saw men in business suits and women in beautiful dresses with smiling faces as they climbed fearlessly into those aerial monsters.

I wandered around, observing all the unfamiliar activities of an airport. I went by a restaurant with large windows overlooking the ramp and the runways. Many of those fearless and attractive people were having breakfast. Ah, the scrumptious smells that found their way to my nose. They reminded me of my hunger and the reason why I was there. I went back to the task at hand—finding Commander Cora.

I inquired where to find Commander Cora's office and, with apprehension, I headed that way. I couldn't get the courage to ask for him. I sat in the waiting room for about an hour, thinking I shouldn't be there, that it was a waste of time, and that I was very hungry. A secretary walked by me several times. When she finally asked whom I was waiting to see, I told her Commander Cora.

She asked my name, left the room, and then came back a few minutes later. She led me to a large office, where a man sat behind a desk. His benevolent smile gave me some confidence, but I quickly lost it when he got up. He was over six feet tall and a very imposing individual. I could hardly speak to tell him who I was and why I was there, but I finally blurted out a few words.

"Oh, yes, I remember," he told me. "I met your mother and her friend, Luz Maria, last week. Why don't you come tomorrow to see if I can find something for you to do?"

Come back tomorrow?

I was glad to get out of his office, but at the same time I just knew he was trying to get rid of me. The feeling of hope I had upon being accepted into his office dwindled ever so slightly. It was like so many other postponements I had experienced in the previous weeks of job searching: "Come back tomorrow" or "Come back next week." The discouragement of the situation reared its ugly head once again, threatening to rob me of my optimism. I had to walk back to the city, which took about three hours. By the time I got back to our room, I had convinced myself that pursuing a job with Commander Cora would be a waste of time.

My mother asked me that night how the job interview had gone. She was sure I was going to tell her that Commander Cora had found something for me to do. I told her it had been a waste of time, just like the many other things I had attempted during the previous weeks. I had been offered a job for seven pesos per week as a "gofer" by a group of drawing artists and photographers who sold cartoons and short illustrated stories to several magazines. I thought the offer was an insult, but getting seven pesos per week was beginning to sound very good. Seven pesos would mean eating for at least three days!

Despite my feelings otherwise, my mother insisted I go back the next day and see Commander Cora. She was sure he would find me a job that would pay a lot more than seven pesos per week. She had gotten a job at a nightclub selling cigarettes and cigars from table to table. She didn't like it, but it paid for the room and for at least one meal a day.

The next day dawned, and I found myself heading to the airport again, against my will. I had to wait half a day before I could see Commander Cora. When he finally had time, he gave me a big smile.

"How about coming back tomorrow, okay?" he said as he was giving his secretary some instructions, and then he disappeared.

Tomorrow, again?

I had a long walk home yet again. I was hungry, tired, disappointed, and very much discouraged. After that experience, I was even more convinced that this airport thing would never amount to anything but a waste of time—time I desperately needed to find a job that provided enough money to eat and help out with the living expenses.

When I got to our room, my mother had already left to go to work until one in the morning, so I was spared the questions regarding my meeting with Commander Cora. I left the following morning before she woke up and went to tell the group of drawing artists that I accepted their offer to work for them for seven pesos a week. I started right away. They used me for whatever they wanted: to make coffee, clean up messes, go get food for them. Occasionally they would let me do some interesting things, such as helping in the dark room developing film. They also had me fill out the black squares in crossword puzzles, which were done by hand in those days.

It was about a week before my mother realized that I was working at that place instead of going to the airport. When she did find out, she was glad to know there was a little more money coming in, but she still thought I could do better at the airport. She insisted I go once more to talk to Commander Cora. Just to please her, I got up at about five o'clock one morning to go to the airport, before reporting to work at the studio.

When I got to the airport, his secretary told me that Commander Cora was flying and that I might be able to see him at one of the hangars by the runway. She told me I could get there by walking all the way around on the perimeter road. It seemed like just another waste of time, but I decided to give it a try since it would be my last time going to the airport to look for work. I figured I might as well explain to Commander Cora how badly I needed a job and how difficult it was to come out to the airport only to be told to come back another day. I had it all rehearsed in my mind, and I wasn't afraid of him anymore—at least when I wasn't in front of him.

I finally arrived at the spot where I was told Commander Cora's airplane would taxi after landing. I waited about thirty minutes, until I saw a small airplane coming in for a landing. This was a little airplane, nothing like the monsters I had seen at the terminal. After completing its landing roll, the airplane headed for the area where I was standing. It made a sharp turn in front of me and came to a stop. With the engine still running, I saw the right door open and Commander Cora get out. He motioned for me to come to him. I approached cautiously. I heard him say something, but I couldn't hear exactly what he said because of the engine noise and the prop-wash blowing on us. By his motions, I understood that I was supposed to get in the airplane and sit in the same seat he had occupied—next to the pilot. As I sat in the tiny cockpit, he secured the seat belt across my lap and closed the door. *Well, this is interesting,* I thought.

I didn't know what was happening. The first thing that came to my mind was that the pilot was going to taxi to the hangar, and maybe I would have to clean it. Could that be the "great" job Commander Cora had found for me? As I was considering that possibility, I noticed that the pilot was not taxiing toward the hangars; instead, he was taxiing to the end of the runway. All of a sudden, my thinking process changed from that of job possibilities to panic!

What is this man doing? I think he is going to attempt to get this … this thing in the air! No … I can't do that! Only "super people" can go up in the air, not me! I don't want to … I … I'm afraid. But he is doing it!

I heard the engine rev up, the tiny machine started to pick up speed, and I closed my eyes. I was sure this was the end of my life. The loud noise continued; very soon I felt a strange sensation, but I felt like I was still alive. I opened one eye as the airplane was making a turn. Then I looked down and everything was getting smaller. I could see little trees and little cars far below me, and the sensation was unbelievable! While floating in the air, I was still alive. I could see farther than I had ever seen.

All too soon the flight ended. I'm sure that Commander Cora had asked the pilot to give the kid a ride "to get him out of his hair," and since he was the commander, the pilot must have thought it was good politics. But he wasn't going to overdo it and burn a lot of gas. The flight couldn't have lasted more than five minutes. The pilot got the airplane on the ground, taxied back to where he had picked up a hungry, scared kid with no aim in life, and told me to get off.

That day I had money to ride the bus back to the city. I sat in the near-empty bus with only one thought in my mind: flight. I could not get the feeling of soaring above it all out of my mind. Despite my hunger and past disappointments, hope swelled in me again, and a dream was born in me.

Now I knew what I wanted to do with my life!

I now had a purpose beyond survival. All the trials and tribulations we were going through seemed trivial compared with the experience I had just had. I kept reliving that short flight over and over in my mind. I looked at the other people riding in the bus and thought, *You poor earthlings, you probably have never been off the ground as I have.* I belonged up there. Before my experience with flight, I had no idea what I wanted to be. But right then and there, I knew I was going to be a pilot.

From then on, nothing could keep me away from the airport. I would spend entire days helping the mechanics by handing them tools, running errands, and washing airplanes. I was driven by a hope that was nurtured far beyond my circumstance, and I couldn't do enough to satiate my new passion. Even though I didn't have any money, there was a kind lady who sold sandwiches and gave me one almost every day. That truly saved my life.

In payment for all the work I did around the airport, the flight instructors would take me up occasionally and teach me some of the basics about the art of flying. It wasn't very often, so my learning process was rather slow. Between flights, I tried to learn as much as I could about what made an airplane fly. Whenever I wasn't busy running errands or helping the mechanics, I would sit in the parked airplanes and examine all the instruments, while reviewing in my mind what the instructors had told me about them: altimeter, air speed indicator, vertical speed indicator, artificial horizon, turn and bank indicator, tachometer. There were also many other instruments and controls that looked so imposing and so beautiful. I would touch each and every one, and I *dreamed*. I had a hope of flying, and that was enough, although I wondered how I would ever achieve my dreams.

There was so much to flying and learning to operate the planes. I watched all the wealthy flight students that came to learn to fly in the airplanes—the very airplanes I washed and helped maintain. They had to spend hours in the classrooms of the "Escuela de Vuelo Mexico" learning about aerodynamics, engines, flight controls, flight maneuvers, electrical systems, hydraulic systems, navigation, and meteorology. They had to be wealthy, as the cost was so great. How would I ever learn all that? How could I ever afford to pay for that training?

The *hope* of flying continued to help me survive, despite our declining situation and although my dream seemed distant and unattainable. I would alternate days at the airport and days at the drawing studio, so I could bring home a little money. It wasn't enough, so we still went without eating for one or two days, sometimes three. With my dreams about flying, I was able to survive without thinking much about it. *Okay, so today I won't eat. No matter, I'll read about flying.* My dream of becoming a pilot was what truly kept me alive. Hope elevated me past my circumstances to a place where anything was possible. When you have hope, you can endure any hardship, any disappointment, and trial. *Live your life with hope!*

Questions

1. The quote by Hal Lindsey at the beginning of the chapter states, "Man can live about forty days without food, about three days without water, about eight minutes without air ... but only for one second without hope." Do you believe this to be true?

2. Have you ever been in a situation that seemed bleak but were able to push through it with hope for a better tomorrow? Give an example from your own life.

3. The author describes the awe he felt when he first visited the airport terminal. He just walked around and looked at everything, feeling very small and insignificant. What situation or circumstance in your life makes you feel insignificant? How can you turn that feeling of "smallness" into a feeling of wonder as the author did?

4. On the third and final visit to Commander Cora, the author was given a ride on an airplane that thrilled him and gave him hope for a brighter future. That airplane ride even solidified his purpose in life and made it possible to persist through hard work, trials, disadvantages, and crippling hunger. Do you have a hope for something better? If you could quantify it, what would that hope be?

5. Dreams may seem trivial to us in the twenty-first century, but they were absolutely vital to the survival of a hungry little boy in Mexico. Dreams can propel you forward and help you achieve your goals. They can "keep you alive" as they did for the author. Write down a dream you have on paper. What steps can you take to make that dream a reality?

Life Lesson #3

Live Your Life with RESOLVE

"When everything seems to be going against you, remember that the airplane takes off against the wind, not with it."

—Henry Ford

Our situation was not improving, even though we were still together as a family and had each other for comfort. We were still barely eating and hardly getting by. Then, as if what we were going through wasn't enough, our situation became suddenly and immeasurably worse.

One day when I got home, my sister had a strange look on her face. I knew something was terribly wrong. Without much hesitation, she told me that our mother had been arrested and put in jail. My heart sank, right then and there. With all that we were going through, how could we accept this terrifying blow that she was in jail? It was a horrible night! In addition to the hunger, we now had the added burden of worrying about our mother, wondering how she was being treated, and imagining all kinds of terrible things that children shouldn't have to worry about.

My sister told me what she knew about the situation. Mother had overheard a conversation between Luz Maria and her boyfriend concerning the assassination of a famous political leader. My mother didn't think much about it, even when she heard that the boyfriend was going to be driving the getaway car.

She figured it was all a hoax. Mother told my sister, but she didn't think she should tell me about it.

One morning, a few days after my mother had heard the conversation, the newspaper headlines read, ATTEMPTED ASSASSINATION LEAVES ONE WOMAN DEAD AND SEVERAL PEOPLE BADLY INJURED. GUNMEN GET AWAY IN BLACK BUICK SEDAN. Apparently the person they were trying to kill escaped unharmed.

When my mother was talking to a lawyer friend a few days later, she hinted that she knew about the assassination attempt. He told her he would give her ten thousand pesos if she gave him all the details, and he promised that she would not be involved. The ten thousand pesos seemed like a fortune to her, especially under our circumstances, and she told him everything she knew.

It turned out to be an unfortunate decision. The police had picked up all the participants in the crime. This included my mother, whom they considered a participant since she hadn't notified the police prior to the assassination attempt. It didn't matter that she hadn't believed the plans were real. Her lawyer friend, who gained a lot of prestige for being the one who caught the criminals, completely abandoned my mother to her fate. She never heard from him again, nor of the ten thousand pesos.

My sister and I continued our daily activities as best we could, while still burdened with the constant worry of not knowing what was happening to our mother. We neither saw nor heard from her. We were determined to press on with our daily responsibilities, but the fear of the unknown put a strain on us both.

My sister finally went to see another lawyer my mother had known for quite some time and told him the whole story. Jose Castro Brito, a jovial young lawyer from Merida, Yucatan, immediately went to see her and assured us that she would be out soon. It was still several days before she was released. It was a great relief to have her home again, but now she lived in constant fear of all the people she had betrayed by divulging what she knew.

When we found ourselves being harassed by the people who were involved with the assassination attempt, she decided it was time to ask her youngest brother to take me to live with him and his wife, even though Mother never wanted to bother her relatives with our problems. My Uncle Joel and his wife lived in the town of Tequila, in the state of Jalisco, near Guadalajara.

I had mixed emotions about going to live with my Uncle Joel. On the one hand, it made sense for my sister and me to get out of Mexico City, since the people who were trying to get even with my mother could have very well retaliated against us. Just as important, it would help us get out of the conditions we were living in. On the other hand, I did not want to leave my mother or be away from airplanes.

We had been through so much tragedy as a family during the last six months, but at least I had my family with me, and the joy of working around airplanes. I still had the dream in my heart to be a pilot one day, and I was determined I would do anything I could to make that happen.

My uncle finally came to Mexico City and convinced me to go back to Tequila with him. At first, it was nice to be living with my Uncle Joel and his family. It was great to eat three times a day and to be around his wife's relatives, who were very wealthy and treated me like one of the family. My Uncle Joel's in-laws were in the business of producing tequila, the famous Mexican liquor. They had two distilleries that produced about 50 percent of the tequila consumed around the world.

During my time with Uncle Joel, I was exposed to all the activities of producing tequila. My uncle supervised some of the activities at the two distilleries, and I had a chance to get involved with every phase of the process, from loading the trucks that transported the mescal to bottling and labeling the finished product. It was an adventure, and it made me feel I was earning my keep. My uncle and I became very close. He was more like a brother than an uncle. He had a great sense of humor, and he made life very pleasant for most everyone around him, including me.

My uncle and his in-laws treated me very well. However, I had tasted flight, and I felt I was wasting time. Every day that went by was one more day that I didn't spend near an airplane or flying in one. I *had* to get back to Mexico City. I was determined to live my dream of becoming a pilot. I was resolved to finish what I had started.

When I told my uncle that I wanted to go back and why, he told me, "You are just dreaming. You can't learn to fly without finishing your education first. You don't have the money. And the situation is very difficult for your mother right now." He was truly concerned about my welfare and tried to convince me it was foolish to go back under the circumstances. But I had made up my mind. I wanted to fly, and Mexico City was the only place I knew where I could be close to airplanes. I felt it was a step I had to take.

My resolve to fulfill my dream led me to have the courage to give up the security of being with my uncle and go back to Mexico City—back to the world of hunger, uncertainty, and airplanes. I was almost fifteen years old, and I just *knew* I would learn to fly and that I would be a commercial pilot someday. I just knew it. Nothing was going to stop me.

* * *

When I got back to Mexico City, the situation had gotten worse for my mother. There had been an attempt to kill her by poisoning her and leaving her out in the countryside for dead. Somehow she was able to walk to a road, and a motorist picked her up and took her to a hospital, where her stomach was pumped. Fearing another attempt on her life, she decided that she needed to leave Mexico City. She went on to Guadalajara, and my sister went to live with our real father in California.

I found myself playing the old game of renting rooms in boardinghouses and moving out when I couldn't pay the rent. I worked at the drawing studio as much as possible, and the rest of the time I was at the airport.

Since my return from Tequila, I had had several encounters with Commander Cora, even though I never went back to him for the purpose of obtaining a job. Now I saw him as the one person whose influence had changed my life, although I never revealed that to him. For some unknown reason, he started treating me differently than he had in the past. Now he would take time to ask me about what I was learning, and he would even impart some of his flying knowledge to me. Even though he had an authoritative personality, most of his subordinates liked him. He was one of the few people who were very supportive of my efforts to learn about aviation, and he was impressed with my perseverance and dogged resolve.

When a rumor started that he was my father, everyone began calling me "Corita," for young Cora. I didn't mind the rumors because I respected him. But Commander Cora surprised me by asking if I would like him to adopt me. I was pleased with the prospect of being Commander Cora's son, so I told him yes, and he started the legal action required for the adoption. While we were waiting for all the formalities, I began to think about the fact that I would soon lose my identity. I wouldn't be Donald Smith anymore; I would be Donald Cora. Somehow it didn't seem right. I had a sense that I was going to lose more than my name. I had begun to enjoy making my own decisions and was proud of the accomplishment of surviving by my own means.

I knew I had to tell Commander Cora I had changed my mind about the adoption. When I told him my decision, he was noticeably disappointed. I knew he truly cared about me. He admonished me that I was throwing away a great opportunity. With him, I would receive all the necessary flight instruction and could go back to school and continue my education.

I knew in my head that he was right about all those things, and I was probably crazy for not accepting his generous and sincere offer, but in the end my gut feeling was that I did not want to go through with the adoption. My heart told me no. He finally said that he respected my decision and wished me luck.

I continued the routine of going to the airport at every opportunity. I would be there from early in the morning until dark, and I did anything I was asked to do. As always, after several days of menial tasks, I was rewarded with twenty or twenty-five minutes of flying time at the end of the day. What a thrill! Everything I had learned on the previous flight, a week or two before, would come back, and I would build on it. One day I would practice turns. I remember the instructor shouting, "Watch your altitude! You're climbing; you're descending. Watch your bank angle! You are losing air speed; add power!"

It was music to my ears.

I had never felt more alive, and I was eager to learn. I would respond to every command and felt the improvement in my overall skill to make the airplane do what I wanted it to do. All too soon it was time to go back to the airport because it was getting dark. This was the part I enjoyed the most, the approach and landing. The instructors were beginning to show me how to land. I would follow the instructor on the dual controls, but I felt as though I were doing it myself. We landed the plane, another flight became history, and I would go back to the world of menial tasks, hunger, and daydreaming.

Life continued for me in the big city without much hope for a solution to my financial problems. I felt foolish for not accepting Commander Cora's offer to adopt me, but I had made the decision and I didn't waste time wondering about how it could have been. My goals continued to keep my dream alive, and I resolved to see them through to completion. I was tempted to wonder "what might have been," but I girded myself with the familiar feeling of determination and resolved to continue working, striving, and learning everything I could to make my dream a reality. When you live with resolve, you are not tempted to allow your dreams to be derailed by even potentially good things. Know what you want in life and have the resolution to see it through. *Live your life with resolve!*

Questions

1. The author made a conscious decision to leave the comforts of living with his Uncle Joel to go back to Mexico City, just so he could follow his dreams. He knew it meant that he would go hungry again and have to fight to survive. Can you identify with that kind of unyielding resolve? How?

2. How do you think resolve can be developed in someone who has not had it modeled for them by family members or friends?

3. Think of the goals and dreams you have for your life. What would you be willing to sacrifice, if anything, to achieve those goals?

4. Is it even possible to reach a goal without some kind of sacrifice? Support your answer with examples from your own life.

5. Make a list of the situations in your life in which you intend to be more resolved. These don't have to be big life goals—they can be small, everyday problems if that is where you struggle.

Life Lesson #4

Live Your Life with a THIRST FOR KNOWLEDGE

"An investment in knowledge pays the best interest."

—Ben Franklin

The promise of flight made everything bearable. As I was cleaning up after everyone at the art studio, or washing airplanes at the airport, or handing tools to the mechanics, or spending the day without eating, my mind was reviewing every maneuver I had practiced the last time I had flown. My mind craved any knowledge that would lead to the achievement of my dream. Unfortunately, the interval between flights was often two or three weeks, so I was limited to this kind of mental repetition of the basics of flight. Because daily flying is so crucial during the early stages of instruction, I believe my mental repetition exercise worked to actually replace the physical mechanics of learning to fly.

Life continued on with a familiar rhythm. I would work one day at the art studio, and I would spend the next day at the airport. Sometimes I would work at the studio in the morning and go to the airport in the afternoon until dark. Everything revolved around making sure I had the opportunity to learn to do what I loved, and that meant spending as much time as possible at the airport. There was nothing that mattered more to me.

It was all part of my plan to achieve my goal of becoming a commercial pilot. I set my sights on that goal, and nothing could change my course. Even hunger did not derail me. I would eat two or three days and go without eating one or two days, with an occasional free torta from the kind woman at the airport. All my energy and desires were focused on that goal. Of course, at the time I didn't realize the harm I was causing to any other possible endeavors. I had embarked on a course of action that would *only* lead to flying, nothing else.

If I had known that the odds were severely stacked against me in my quest, I suppose I would have continued on that course of action anyway. It honestly wasn't a very practical plan at all. It would have made more sense to prepare myself for an alternate career, but it never occurred to me. In my optimistic way of looking at life, I knew I would eventually be a commercial pilot … and not just any commercial pilot, but the best commercial pilot in the world!

One particular instructor among all the others who worked at the Escuela Mexicana de Aviación showed more interest in teaching me to fly. Eleodoro Jimenez was about thirty-five years old, imposing at six feet tall, and always wore khaki pants and shirt and Ray Ban sunglasses. His persona was veiled in mystery, as he watched calmly from behind his sunglasses and never got excited. In situations when other instructors would shout louder than necessary, he would just raise his voice to overcome the engine and wind noise and say exactly the right thing to make me correct whatever mistake I had made.

There was no official agreement with the flight school about giving me anything in return for my labors; even though the mechanics appreciated my help, they were in no position to offer me anything in return. I was too timid and shy to request any kind of payment for my labor, so I just worked at whatever I could find, hoping that someone would notice and reward me with those few precious minutes of flying time I received once in a while.

Mr. Jimenez was one of those who noticed my efforts and my desire to learn to fly. On those occasions when he asked me if I wanted to go up, I would drop whatever I was doing and run to the airplane to get it ready. He would sit under one of the wings, and with the aid of a stick, etch in the dirt our flight plans for that day.

I soaked up every word he said like a sponge. My mind thrilled to each and every word he spoke, because I knew that learning from him was an amazing opportunity. He was one of the best instructors in the school. I felt so important. Nothing else mattered in my life but to absorb every word that came out of his mouth.

Our flight lesson soon began, and I proceeded with the preliminary flight measures. When I yelled, "Contact!" he would put both hands on the propeller, give it a crank, and the little engine would start with the sweetest sound—it was like music to my ears. Coming around and getting in the backseat, Mr. Jimenez would signal that we were ready to go. He would then talk me through the taxiing, the run-up, and the takeoff. What a thrill! I could feel his sure movements on the dual controls.

Then came the moment when the controls wouldn't move unless I moved them. I came to life! This is where I belonged. While reviewing the maneuvers we had discussed, Mr. Jimenez would constantly drill me on how to improve my coordination of the controls and the smooth but quick use of power. Before I knew it, the time had come to return to the airport, and I had learned a few more things about the art of flying. I lived for those moments.

Knowledge Is not Always Wisdom

Some of my learning opportunities came in more unconventional forms. In addition to the "official" flying lessons that I received sporadically, some of the rich playboys who kept their airplanes at the school hangars would take me up to flaunt their flying skills. One of those playboys, whose nickname was "Super Loco," tried to live up to his moniker. He was a master of the art of buzzing—flying fast and close to the ground (he called it *el sagrado borraceo*, the sacred buzzing). As soon as we left the traffic pattern, he would descend to just above the ground and accelerate to the airplane's maximum speed, hopping over trees and any other obstructions.

One day we flew over the highway that goes to the town of Puebla. He aligned the airplane with the road and dove toward the surface at maximum speed as he aimed directly for a car coming in the opposite direction. It was a game of chicken. He waited until the last second before pulling the nose up to climb over the car. I saw the driver's eyes almost come out of their sockets as we almost collided. From the back seat I could hear Super Loco laughing with maniacal glee. I could not understand his cavalier attitude toward learning to fly. It was a privilege to soar above the earth, and I could never imagine jeopardizing my opportunity to learn by behaving with such carelessness.

I flew with Super Loco one more time, to the floating gardens of Xochimilco, where he practiced the same recklessness he had displayed over the highway near Puebla. As we were heading back to the airport, I promised myself I would never go up with him again. I never had the chance to turn him down, because he killed himself shortly after the Xochimilco escapade, doing a series of thirteen loops. He struck the ground coming out of the thirteenth.

I was greatly affected by the death of Super Loco. It was the first time in my life that I was directly exposed to the death of someone I knew, and it was also my first recognition of the fact that aviation could kill you. I had some moments of apprehension and doubts about whether I wanted to continue pursuing a career in aviation. I went to the rooming house that night in a very somber mood. I stayed away from the airport for a couple of days, contemplating what I wanted to do with my life. I also pondered the reality of death.

When I confided in the studio photographer that I was fearful of the reality that people can get killed in airplanes, he had a very wise reply for me: "It is harder for us to lose someone when he or she dies than for us to die. And some people are so afraid to die that they never begin to live."

I kept thinking about my conversation with him the rest of that day. The realization began to grow in me that I could treat my knowledge of aviation with the respect it deserved, and I would be far less apt to suffer the same fate as Super Loco. Just because someone has the knowledge needed to be successful does not mean they have the wisdom to use it prudently.

With my fear abated and my dream rejuvenated, I was ready to go back to the airport the next morning as determined as ever to continue with my plans to learn to fly. Only this time, I knew I had to learn all the intricacies, so I could be a safe pilot in addition to being the best. There is a saying that there are old pilots, and there are bold pilots, but there are no old, bold pilots.

My Education Continues on the Ground

One foggy morning when it was impossible to fly, Mr. Jimenez was sitting on a fence trimming his fingernails while waiting for the fog to burn off. Sitting by him, I confessed that I really didn't feel I was learning what I needed to know to fly an airplane. He spent the next few hours, until the fog cleared, explaining the mechanics of flight in simple terms for me, using the dirt on the ground as illustration. I imagined all of the flights I had completed with him, and my mind worked overtime to assimilate all of the information he was communicating.

The fog finally lifted, and our lesson ended. But as I headed to my post on the runway to direct traffic, it all began to make sense. It was all coming together. Like placing another puzzle piece in its place, my mind fit the information I had just learned about the mechanics of lift and stalls in the grand scheme of learning to fly.

Each little tidbit I gleaned from my time with Mr. Jimenez was more valuable to me than gold. I was very grateful for his willingness to explain everything to me. I knew that he had no obligation to do so since I was not an official flight student, yet he treated me as if I were his most prized pupil. From then on, I was always on the lookout for times when I could get a little more knowledge from him or any of the other instructors. I never stopped craving just one more lesson or one more flight plan to add to my skills. My thirst for knowledge was part of the driving force that ultimately led me to achieve my dreams. When you live with a thirst for knowledge, your classroom can be anywhere! You will soak up information from anywhere it is presented to you. Never stop learning in order to reach your dreams. *Live your life with a thirst for knowledge!*

Questions

1. The author states that he believes his faithful mental repetition of the basics of flight served as a substitution for actual flight time, even though flight time is considered very important, especially early on in the learning process. Do you think this practice of mental repetition would apply to some area of your life (school, job training, positive affirmations, etc.)?

2. When other options are taken away from us (or abandoned by us), our focus on any remaining goal is exponentially increased. This is what happened for the author. Can you imagine what would happen if you abandoned all but your most important goals? Do you think you would be more likely to achieve them if you didn't have to worry about less important things? Give examples from your own life.

3. The author faced the death of a pilot whom he admired, even though that pilot behaved recklessly. This experience caused him to question his dream of learning to fly because of the potential danger and served as a major setback. Share a time in your life where you questioned your choices or goals because of the real, or imagined, negative consequences.

4. The studio photographer said, "Some people are so afraid to die that they never begin to live." Have you seen this fear manifested in your life? Explain.

5. The author attributed his time with Mr. Jimenez as being instrumental to his learning the basics of flight. Mr. Jimenez believed in the author's potential and spent time teaching him, despite the fact that he was not an official student. Think of someone in your life that has served to inspire you

in this manner, despite what you may have perceived as your own shortcomings.

Life Lesson #5

Live Your Life with FINESSE

"When love and skill work together, expect a masterpiece."

—Charles Reade

It was great to get back to the airport. I hadn't really noticed how colorful it was. There were yellow airplanes all over the tie-down areas—Piper Cubs, Aeronca Champions, and Fleets. The school was a beehive of activity. Little yellow airplanes were taxiing all over the dirt and grass parking and taxi areas. Since none of the surfaces were paved, they were rather rough, and the airplanes seemed to wave their wings as their wheels rolled over the uneven ground.

As I observed all the activity, I began to feel alive again, and I was anxious to get airborne. If only I could. I went directly to Mr. Jimenez and told him about all my fears and doubts. I also told him that I had gotten over them, and I was ready to start flying again.

"So that's why you haven't been around," he said. "I've looked for you, because I've been thinking that you need to fly more often at this stage of your training. The first few times we went up together, I didn't really know if you were serious about learning. After seeing you work the way you do, just to be around airplanes, and noticing your progress during the few flights you've taken, I'm sure you have the potential to become a good pilot."

I didn't know what to say, or whether to laugh or cry. Hearing those words from a man whom I considered the best flight instructor in the Escuela Mexicana de Aviación was like a dream come true! I wanted to say, "Yes! Yes! I know I will be the best pilot in the world."

But all I said was, "Thank you, but I don't have the money."

He shrugged and told me that we would just continue doing what we had been doing, except he would try to take me up every day instead of once a week or whenever we could. He told me that we would be working with the regular school syllabus as well.

I was speechless. What a wonderful feeling! All the rest of that day and late into the night, I was picturing myself in the cockpits of either a Piper Cub, or the Aeronca, or even the Fleet, for I had just gotten a ride in a Fleet shortly before Super Loco's accident.

The next day, I arrived at the airport around seven in the morning. I knew we wouldn't be able to fly until the end of the day, but I just couldn't wait. Mr. Jimenez was walking to an airplane with one of his students; he called me over, gave me the school syllabus, and told me to be prepared for lesson one.

I sat in the backseat of an airplane that wasn't being used and started reading. I felt on top of the world. The syllabus included basics like preflight and straight and level flight, as well as advanced maneuvering—like spins and turns.

At last I was on course with a plan and a direction! Now I knew what I was going to be doing, and finally things made sense. I still couldn't believe that all this was happening to me. But it was happening, and I had to start studying.

Learning Finesse in Flight

I read all about "Familiarization and Control Operation" and quickly determined that I already knew just about everything in the chapter. One interesting paragraph read: "The airplane is so designed that it is stable in the air, control forces are light, and the controls must be *smoothly and positively used*. The grip on the stick or wheel should be comfortably firm but relaxed to obtain the proper reaction."

I had learned this principle the hard way. Since I hadn't been told about this characteristic, my first attempts at controlling an airplane had been rather jerky, for I was doing exactly the opposite of what I was just reading; I would hold the stick so tightly that I'm sure my knuckles turned white. I remembered one time when Mr. Jimenez's lady friend, who was an instructor pilot too, took me up for one of my flights late in the day.

She told me I was holding the controls too tightly, and she had a novel way of retraining me. She told me to take my feet off the pedals. (The rudder pedals are directly behind the front seat of the airplane). I did as she directed. Then she put her hands on the pedals and told me to put my feet back on the pedals again, which meant putting my feet on the backs of her hands.

"You don't want to hurt my hands, do you?" she asked. "Okay then, let's make a turn; as you are coordinating the use of the rudder with the movement of the ailerons, be gentle and don't hurt my hands."

What a lesson! It taught me to relax, and it showed me that there was some finesse involved with flying, especially if I wanted to fly smoothly. My dream was beginning to take shape.

Becoming a Smooth Operator

Mr. Jimenez and I went up that first day of "official" flying lessons, and the task was to fly straight and level. Simple, I thought. I even thought it was a waste of time. I wanted to learn *more advanced* maneuvers. What I didn't realize was that flying straight and level is not as simple as it sounds.

When he gave me the airplane, after demonstrating what straight and level flight looked like, I committed just about every error most students commit during this task: I was rough on the controls, I flew with one wing low, I gained and lost altitude, and I couldn't keep a constant heading. It was embarrassing. Not very smooth either. I could see it was going to be a long road ahead. With his patience and ability to say the right thing at the right time, by the time we got back that evening I was doing a very good job of keeping the airplane at a fixed altitude, heading, and air speed.

We continued with the syllabus, and I studied the manual with ferocity in order to prepare for my next lesson. I read that proper application of the rudder was crucial to avoid the tendency of the airplane to yaw toward the high wing when banking and to achieve a smooth, coordinated turn entry. I also had to keep in mind the up elevator pressure necessary throughout the turn and any extra lift required through adding power and speed. The name of the game was coordination.

Armed with this information, I was ready for my next flight, which came as a surprise early in the morning. Normally we couldn't get an airplane until late in the day. Mr. Jimenez couldn't always get an airplane on a daily basis without having to pay for it, so there were days when I didn't fly. But I still got my lessons more frequently, and they were better organized than the previous haphazard exposure to flying I had experienced.

The weather was perfect! Clear, no wind, and just right for what I needed to practice. I knew that I was ready to apply my book knowledge and hard-earned flight finesse to my next lesson. I was prepared to fly with the potential that Mr. Jimenez expected of me and get that much closer to my dream.

When you live with finesse, it means handling situations, circumstances, or problems with skill rather than with sheer strength. Just like putting a little pressure on the controls helped me to direct a large plane, a little adjustment here and there in your life can help you to get that much closer to your dreams. *Live your life with finesse!*

Questions

1. The author, because of his determination and having proved his resolution to Mr. Jimenez, was finally able to take real flight lessons. He poured himself into the manual, even though he knew some of the material from actual flight experience. What areas of your life (parenting, leadership, job performance, etc.) could you possibly perform better if you "went back to the basics?"

2. The author recounts the story of how he learned the importance of flying with finesse from an instructor who made him use the pedals with her hands on top of them. He learned to control the plane more effectively by letting go a bit and using less force, even though it seemed counterintuitive. How can we relate this concept of "better control through letting go" to our lives?

3. Often in life, a soft touch or a bit more compassion is required to be successful. Can you think of any examples of compassion that were more effective than being subjected to a tirade or other form of negative consequence? For example, maybe a teacher gave you a second chance to turn in a paper, or a manager pulled you aside privately to admonish you rather than yelling at you in front of everyone. What was your attitude after that more compassionate gesture?

4. When wanting to jump ahead to more advanced maneuvers, the author learned that the "easy" things—in this case, flying straight and level—are not always as simple as they sound. What "easy" things have you been challenged with lately? Explain.

5. When the author was studying flight turns in his manual, he was astounded by the many factors that came into play in

order to execute a smooth turn. "The name of the game is coordination." We may call this multitasking in our modern culture. How can you use finesse in your life to stay coordinated, even when multiple factors are in play (e.g., using a calendar, task list, etc.)?

Life Lesson #6

Live Your Life with WORTH

"You will be as much value to others as you have been to yourself."

—Marcus T. Cicero

I was almost sixteen years old, and flying was in my blood. I was no stranger to hard work, but my living conditions hadn't improved. I was still looking for a way to earn some money, so when I heard about a job at the CMAPEFA (Comisión México Americana para la Erradicación de la Fiebre Aftosa) I was open to it. This was a commission that had been formed in partnership with the U.S. government to deal with the alarming spread of hoof-and-mouth disease in cattle before it reached the United States.

The organization was looking for bilingual personnel, eighteen years of age or older, for immediate positions in their many departments. My first reaction was, *I am only sixteen, and I don't speak English. There's no use in even trying to apply for a job in the CMAPEFA. But, then again, what do I have to lose?* I pushed aside any fears and decided to go for it. I knew I could do a good job if I was given the chance to prove myself.

I filled out the required forms (advancing my age two years) and met with a lady who immediately asked me, "Do you speak Spanish?" in English. When I nodded, she immediately switched to Spanish, and I proceeded to impress her with my knowledge of the Spanish language. She didn't revert back to English, so I'm sure she must have assumed that I spoke English because of my name. She didn't question my age; after making a few entries on the form, she sent me to another part of the building where I was notified that I had been hired! My salary was going to be two hundred fifty pesos per month, and I had to report for work the following morning. Two hundred fifty pesos was equivalent to twenty-nine dollars, but it was a fortune to me!

I poured myself into my work at the CMAPEFA in the information department. Our task was to educate the public about hoof-and-mouth disease and to inform them that the infected cattle had to be killed. It was a very busy place and always challenging. We made use of radio stations and newspapers to disseminate the information throughout the parts of the Mexican Republic where the disease was more prevalent.

Flying had to be put on hold for a while because I didn't have the time to go to the airport, and I didn't feel right about getting the free flying without working for it. After a few months, however, I did manage to go to the airport during the weekends and sometimes early in the morning or late in the afternoon. Mr. Jimenez continued giving me as much flight instruction as possible. I finally learned most of the maneuvers in the flying syllabus. It was during one of those afternoons that I had the opportunity to experience my first solo flight, which I related in the beginning of my story. It was glorious. One moment I was on the ground, and the next I was airborne, my fate in my own hands at the controls. My heart soared.

In the same way, my life began to take off as I made my mark on the commission, finding value in my work there. I learned quickly what was expected of me, and I threw myself into it with a lot of enthusiasm. I was so grateful for the opportunity to earn a decent salary that there wasn't anything I would not have done to ensure my continued employment. By the time the organization discovered that I didn't speak English, I had demonstrated my willingness to go the "extra mile." The head of the department overlooked my handicap, and I was given a raise to four hundred pesos per month after three months. My worth in my job was secured.

My outlook on life changed considerably in many ways, first and foremost because I felt the satisfaction of being useful. I guess it was that innate desire we all have of wanting to be of service. I finally felt that I had some worthwhile work and was truly valuable to my employer. Plus, I had been rewarded for my hard work with a raise. I was really living! I had a room in a boardinghouse in a very nice neighborhood, new clothes, and I ate three meals every day. I was also able to send money to my mother who was now living in the city of Guadalajara.

A Worthwhile Surprise

One of my duties with the CMAPEFA was to visit the American Embassy at least once a week to deliver and retrieve information concerning the operation of the commission. During those brief visits I became acquainted with several members of the embassy. One of them was curious about my name, Smith, and asked if I had been born in the United States. When I told him I was born in Mexico and that my father, an American, had left when I was three, he took it upon himself to look through his records, which revealed a surprising discovery. On my following visit, he presented me with an affidavit showing that my father had registered my sister and me as U.S. citizens when we were six and three years of age.

What a great surprise! I didn't know what to say. He then proceeded to tell me that if I wanted to keep my American citizenship I had to go to the United States and register in the Selective Service. Otherwise, I would be drafted in Mexico at age eighteen (which was in twenty days!), and I would lose that right. I didn't know what he was talking about and had no idea what the Selective Service was. What should I do? I left the embassy with a copy of the two affidavits showing that I was an American citizen. It was the most precious gift I could have ever received! I was so thankful to my father for having done that. But then my heart sank as I realized I had to leave Mexico immediately.

My boss, Dr. L.R. Noyes, from Fayetteville, Arkansas—who had also served as a mentor to me—completely understood and agreed that I had to go to the United States. After showing him the certificate of registration and citizenship I had just received, he congratulated me and wished me well.

I spent the next three days getting rid of all the things I couldn't take with me, packing, and notifying the few people I knew that I was starting a new life. I also called my father in California and told him about my plans; he seemed pleased to hear about my decision. He then offered to meet me at the border. It was so strange to be talking to my father. I guess I should have done it before, but it never crossed my mind.

After paying my debts, buying the train ticket and a suitcase, I had two hundred fifty-five pesos (thirty dollars) left to my name. Not much, but the opportunity I had before me was well worth the risk.

On June 29, 1949, I left Mexico City on a train bound for the U.S. and Mexico border at Mexicali and Calexico. The temperature was stifling and the ride uncomfortable, but all I could think about was that I was going to the greatest country in the world and would have the opportunity to learn much more advanced aviation knowledge than was available in Mexico. I could see myself learning more about flying and eventually realizing my dream of becoming a professional pilot. Nothing else mattered.

I arrived in Mexicali on July 2, 1949, in the middle of the desert, since there was no station. Many of the passengers were taking the old taxicabs, but with the little money I had, I chose to walk to my hotel, a simple adobe structure. My father had said he was going to try to get there the same day I was scheduled to arrive, but that he might be one day late. I hoped he would be on time.

I was starting to wash up when I heard a knock on the door. It was my father! I must have been five the last time I had seen him. I really didn't remember him except for some pictures. He was slim and slightly taller than I was, with brown hair and eyes. It was a little awkward at first as we started shaking hands. Then we embraced each other, but we didn't know what to say. We talked about the heat, my trip, and his drive from Glendale. And then we ran out of small talk.

"You'd better pack your things," he said. "We are leaving right away."

My father and I headed for his shiny, late model Chevrolet. I loaded my bag into the trunk and got in the right front seat. I began to feel the difference between where I had been and where I was going.

We stopped at the border, and the inspector asked my father his nationality. I couldn't understand the conversation, but it was obvious that my father was answering some questions from the inspector about me. I had my ID card in my hand, but the inspector didn't ask for it; he just waved us through.

What a feeling! It was like dying and going to heaven. Immediately after leaving the border everything was clean, orderly, and spacious. The highway was perfectly paved and wide. We were gliding along so smoothly that it seemed as if we were on a cloud. As we crossed some small towns, all I could see were neat, little houses with green lawns, just like in the American movies I had seen.

Up until this point in my life, I had found my worth in hard work, determination, and the satisfaction that comes with being valued for your effort. I knew there were many more days of hard work ahead of me, but I knew in my heart that there was great worth just in becoming a U.S. citizen and being a part of the American dream. Perhaps my dreams would be realized as I continued my life's journey in this remarkable place.

When you live with a feeling of worth, you know who you are and who you are capable of becoming. Despite my humble beginnings, I was given the opportunity to start a new life in the greatest country on earth. If I had not had a deep sense of my own worth and the value of living in America, I may have chosen to stay in Mexico and let whatever happened happen. But I knew my worth. You have great worth as well, and you are capable of achieving your dreams. *Live your life with worth!*

Questions

1. The author got a job at the CMAPEFA, despite the fact he was technically not qualified for it (he was too young and could not speak English). He knew that, if given the chance, he could prove his worth to the organization, and he did. In what tangible ways can you express your worth (hard work, determination, willingness to do anything, compassion), despite feeling "unqualified" in certain areas of your life?

2. The author's employment with CMAPEFA may have seemed like a major detour from his dreams, but it eventually led to the surprising discovery of his U.S. citizenship. What major detours have you experienced in the realization of your dream?

3. The author's claim to U.S. citizenship forced him to make the quick decision to leave Mexico for the United States. He was excited at the prospect of living in a country with as much opportunity as America offered. Share a decision you have made in your life that forced you to choose between leaving something good behind for the promise of something better (relationship, job, home, etc.).

4. The author's father had only been a distant thought until he decided to go to the United States to live with him. It served the purpose of giving him a place to live and pushing him to learn English right away, although their relationship was strained. Sometimes we discount people because of past history or our perceptions of them. Share a time when you were surprised by how a person in your life was able to push you closer to your goals.

5. The author had to literally relocate to another country in pursuit of his dream. He was probably still very

uncomfortable being so far from home, in a country where he could not understand the language; he would still have to overcome the language barrier. How far are you willing to go, and how uncomfortable are you willing to get, to make sure you achieve your goals?

Life Lesson #7

Live Your Life with MOTIVATION

"Strength doesn't come from what you can do. It comes from overcoming the things you once thought you couldn't."

—Rikki Rogers

My father and I spent the night in one of the towns with the neatly trimmed lawns and continued toward Glendale, California, the following day, arriving late that night. Despite the long time in the car together, we hadn't spoken to each other much during our trip. I used the silence to contemplate the decision I had made and the hard road that was most likely ahead of me.

When we arrived at my father's home, I met my stepmother. She showed me the way to my room, where an army cot had been outfitted with blankets and sheets, and wished me a good night. I was very excited about being in the United States and thankful that my father and stepmother were willing to help me. But I knew that I had to find a job right away, so I could support myself and eventually live on my own. That was my motivation to acclimate to my new country as quickly as possible.

The next morning was the Fourth of July, 1949. I got up and went to the main house where my father and his family were just about to have breakfast. It was then that I met my four-year-old half-brother, Keith. I said good morning in Spanish, and my father answered in English. Of course, my stepmother also spoke to me in English, pointing to where my place was at the table. Right then and there, I realized that the use of the Spanish language had ceased in that house as of the night before when my father had said good night in Spanish.

I went out to explore the surroundings and take stock of my situation. I continued to be completely overwhelmed, as everything I encountered was beautiful. I was still excited about being in the United States, but I was scared! I felt trapped. How could I possibly find a job without speaking English? How could I do *anything* without knowing the language?

As I was mulling all those things over in my mind, the thought came to me that I must return to Mexico. For a moment, I let fear take hold of me. I didn't think I was capable of learning English, and I didn't feel I had the time it would take to learn the language. Then, as the fear subsided, my reason returned. I thought, *What can I go back to? There is nothing for me in Mexico.*

I made up my mind. I didn't like my situation, nor did I feel welcome at my father's house, but I would stay there while I learned the language. During our drive from Calexico, my father had mentioned that he might be able to get me a job where he worked, and that the local high school offered night courses in English for foreign people.

I started formulating a plan. I would start going to school the following day and hopefully learn enough English to be able to work as soon as possible. I still had many doubts about having the ability to do it, but I just didn't have a choice. I was highly motivated to get myself into a better situation as soon as possible. I knew nothing could stop me once I had made up my mind.

That night, as I watched the Fourth of July fireworks display and celebration in the neighborhood, I felt as if it were a reflection of my own celebration of independence. It certainly was a symbolic way for me to experience the beginning of my life in this new country.

Motivation to Learn English

Instinctively I quit using Spanish completely. I neither spoke, nor read, nor wrote, nor even thought in it. It was one of the most difficult times in my life. I could not communicate! Somehow, I made it to Glendale High School, a three-story brick building, where Mrs. Brandon was teaching an English class for foreign people. With each class I attended, I was like a sponge, absorbing just about everything she taught. I attended her class Mondays, Wednesdays, and Fridays, and on Tuesday and Thursday nights, I went to Hoover High to a remedial English class for high school students. Before I found work, I spent the days studying English and the nights at school learning more.

Within one week, I was able to secure a job at my father's place of work, the General Panel Corporation in Burbank, California, where he was the CFO. The General Panel Corporation built prefabricated houses, and all of the components for the houses were manufactured in the plant. My job was to organize all the necessary hardware for use in an assembly line fashion, as well as various menial duties, since I was really considered a helper in all areas. I was paid two dollars and fifty cents an hour, which I thought was very generous.

I registered with the Selective Service and with the Social Security Administration. Despite my official citizenship, the English language still sounded like machine-gun fire. I couldn't tell when a word ended and the next one began. Nevertheless, I stuck to the total immersion technique of learning a language. I did not attempt, under any circumstance, to use Spanish. I used the few English words I was learning in school as much as possible. I finally got over my shyness, and I spoke to just about anybody I encountered. It was amazing! People would actually stop and help me learn to pronounce words correctly.

One day, about one month after my arrival in the United States, I went to bed not understanding much of what I heard. When I got up the following day and went to the house for breakfast, I understood everything my stepmother said. I understood what my father and stepbrother were saying.

I still couldn't completely express myself, but I could hear when each word ended and the next one began. It was like a miracle! After just thirty days of total immersion, I now understood a new language. I felt confident enough to give up the English class for foreign people and dedicate all my time and energy to the remedial English classes at Hoover High.

Motivation to Fly

With my newfound understanding, I felt ready to go to the local airport, Grand Central at Glendale, and see if I could rent an airplane and continue learning the art of flying. I found a flight instructor, L.G. Chapman, who was willing to check me out in one of their Aeroncas. It was to be my first flight in the U.S. As soon as we started the preflight check of the airplane, I realized that I didn't understand some of the aviation terminology. During our first flight when he told me, "Take off power," I thought he meant to turn the power off. I was mistaken, of course, and I received quite a lecture after Mr. Chapman taxied the airplane back.

I decided I would learn more English before I continued my flying lessons, but that just provided me with more motivation to perfect my understanding of the English language.

In February 1950, I went back to the airport, and after proving to Mr. Chapman that my English had improved considerably, I continued my flying lessons. He gave me about five more hours of flying time before he felt satisfied that I could fly solo again. One morning we flew from Grand Central Airport to Lancaster in the Mojave Desert. After practicing a few landings there, Mr. Chapman got out of the airplane, and I flew solo for the third time in my life. It was almost as enjoyable as the second time.

Motivation to Move On

I never felt welcome in my father's house—in fact, I felt like an outsider. As soon as I had enough money, I began to look for a place to stay. I ended up renting a room with a family of six, the Hoiseths, who had just relocated to California from South Dakota. They gave me room and board for one hundred fifty dollars per month, and I had my own room with very nice furniture and was treated like one of the family.

At just about the same time I moved in with the Hoiseths, there was a reduction in force at the General Panel Corporation and I was laid off. Fortunately, I was able to find work at a nearby lumberyard; that allowed me to continue my routine of working from eight to four, while going to school from six to nine at night. The lumberyard job made it possible for me to continue learning English, to pay for an occasional flying lesson, to pay for room and board, and to send money to my mother. The job was hard work, and sometimes I would fall asleep during class at night. I certainly didn't have anything against hard work, but I felt this occupation was not getting me any closer to the path I needed in order to realize my dream.

I remember saying this to one of my coworkers one day as a B-36 was flying overhead. He just laughed and said, "You are dreaming! It takes a lot of money and education. You'll never make it."

Several other people had expressed this sentiment to me at different times when I confided in them. Of course, remarks like that just made me even more determined to do whatever I needed to achieve my goal. I set my sights on that goal, and I would use all my time and energy to become a professional pilot.

After that, I would not tell just anybody what I wanted to do with my life, because of all the discouraging remarks I had heard. But I felt I wanted to talk to someone about my predicament. So I confided in an old man who lived across the street from the Hoiseths. One day I told him what my goal was, and I admitted that I really didn't know how to achieve it and felt I was wasting time.

"If you want to fly, why don't you join the Air Force?" he asked me.

He told me I might not be able to fly right away, but that I would be closer to airplanes and flying than I was now. That certainly made sense, and I thought about my conversation with the old man for about a week. One day, while I was on my way home, I stopped at a recruiting office. I didn't know what to expect when I went in, but the little sliver of hope that the old man had given me motivated me.

As I walked into the office, I went into a simple structure filled with glass windows and large posters declaring "Join the Air Force." A friendly man in uniform, about thirty-five years old, asked if he could help me. I mentioned to him that I was interested in aviation, and he told me I would need to take some screening tests to determine whether I had the necessary educational background to be accepted into the Air Force. He added that the testing would take about two hours. When I told him I didn't have time, he said I could come back during the weekend if I preferred.

I did return the following Saturday to take the tests. My confidence level was rather low, but I figured nothing would be gained by waiting until I felt better qualified to take the tests. I thought, *If nothing else, I will learn what is expected, and I can prepare myself to take the tests again at a later time.* However, after spending about two and a half hours answering questions, my confidence level rose. When I returned the test papers to the person in charge, I was very confident that I would be accepted.

Sure enough, I received a letter from the recruiting office the following Friday stating that I had passed the screening tests. My confidence soared. If I wanted to join the Air Force, that letter would serve as my authorization to report to the main recruiting office in Los Angeles for a physical examination and the final required testing prior to induction into the Armed Forces of the United States of America.

Talk about mixed emotions! I really didn't know whether I wanted to commit myself to military duty, and I wasn't sure I would even qualify for flight training. I had dozens of other unanswered questions. However, that letter surely revealed an escape from the rut I was in and the possible opportunity for realizing my dream. I had to do it!

On April 13, 1950, I reported to the main recruiting office in Los Angeles. There must have been about fifty other enlistees. We were directed to the medical section of the building for a physical examination; we also filled out countless forms and took more written tests. A team of officers then interviewed us individually; finally, around 4:30 in the afternoon, we were sworn in. I was then a private, or airman in today's United States Air Force.

We were given three days to put our affairs in order, after which we were to report to the same building at 0700 hours, April 17, 1950. The possibilities that this new direction my life was taking overwhelmed my mind. I had just qualified to serve in the U.S. Armed Forces, even though there was much uncertainty. This accomplishment would have never been possible without the consistent motivation that inspired me to move forward.

Despite the language barrier, cultural differences, and feeling like an outsider in a new country, I had gotten one step closer to my dream. I believed in myself, even though I had no one to believe in me and inspire me to go on. When you live your life with motivation, you have a drive to never give up on your dreams, even when you are not sure of the right direction and others doubt you. Find a passion that will motivate you to achieve what others consider impossible. *Live your life with motivation!*

Questions

1. The author shares in the first part of this chapter how isolating it felt to be in a country where no one would speak to him in his native Spanish tongue. Have you ever been in a situation where you felt like an outsider? Explain.

2. How do you feel about his father refusing to speak Spanish to him after his first night in the United States? Do you think they were motivated by concern for him and wanted him to adapt quickly? Why or why not?

3. The author was able to learn the English language in a very short time because of his "immersion" technique of not speaking, thinking, reading, or writing in Spanish. He only used the few English words he knew. To what new desired habit, learning pursuit, or skill could you apply this same technique? Have you ever personally used this learning method?

4. The author relates how many people tried to dissuade him from his dream by telling him he would never make it. He responded to those comments by saying that "remarks like that just made me even more determined to do whatever I needed to achieve my goal." Share either a time when you allowed someone to abandon a dream because of his opinion, or a time when you motivated yourself to keep going despite negative feedback.

5. Leaving the relative safety of his job at the lumberyard, the author joined the Air Force after being told it might help him to achieve his goals, even though there was no guarantee that he would be able to fly. He was so motivated to pursue his dream that he took a chance in

order to have the opportunity to achieve it. Can you share a time when you took a chance that got you closer to your goals?

Life Lesson #8

Live Your Life with EXPECTATION

"Achievement is largely the product of steadily raising one's level of aspiration and expectation."

—Jack Nicklaus

The day after I was sworn into the Air Force, April 14, 1950, I began to get my affairs in order. I honestly wasn't sure I had done the right thing, since everyone I told about my decision thought I had made a big mistake. All I heard were tales of woe. No one gave me a single word of encouragement except the old man across the street from the Hoiseths.

"You'll never regret it," he told me. "The majority of the people who say you shouldn't have done it don't know what they are talking about. Many of them wouldn't have the guts to volunteer as you did. This is one of the best things you could have done with your life. You will be serving your country at the same time you are improving the chances of fulfilling your dream."

I really needed to hear that. My optimism returned, and I felt I had finally discovered the avenue that would lead me to the achievement of my dream. My expectations were high once again.

I notified my employer that I was leaving, attended my last English class, and packed the few things I thought I would need for my next venture. It was 5:30 in the morning on April 17, 1950, when the Hoiseths, who had become like family to me, drove me to the recruiting office in Los Angeles. They dropped me off, and we said our last good-byes. I looked around at the group of men who would be going to Lackland Air Force Base in San Antonio, Texas. There were some tears, hugs, and promises to write. Then a bus pulled up to the curb, and the man in charge of our group started barking orders to board the bus.

During the bus ride to the train station, the enormity of the step I had taken finally began to sink in. Although I was used to making decisions that I stuck to, this was one time when, for a moment, I wished it were a dream. It was obvious that the rest of the recruits in the bus were also apprehensive. However, their way of venting was by joking and telling stories about life in the military. I began to feel the sense of camaraderie that a group feels when they are sharing the same fate. After a wait of about three hours, we finally boarded the train bound for San Antonio, Texas. It was our first lesson in one of the facts about life in the military: hurry up and wait.

The corporal in charge of our group felt it was his duty to start getting us into shape. During the thirty-three hours it took to get to San Antonio, he made sure we understood our new status in life. It was definitely not to enjoy a leisurely trip in the first-class section of the train. He took every opportunity to make sure that we started studying military protocol, as well as several other subjects to do with basic training.

We arrived in San Antonio late in the evening. We got off the train and fell into formation as our corporal marched us outside, where about one hundred other recruits waited to be transported to Lackland Air Force Base. Very soon, several trucks pulled up to the area where we were waiting; we scrambled around until each of us could find room in one of the trucks. The ride to Lackland took about one hour; it was close to midnight when we finally checked in at the processing center.

We were issued our GI clothing, which consisted of two pairs of fatigues, five sets of underwear, five pairs of socks, one pair of brogans, and a duffel bag. From there, we went to a large area where we were given a GI haircut, and then it was on to the showers to clean up. After we had put on our new military clothing, we were marched to the infirmary. Two rows of nurses were waiting as we entered, and they told us to remove the upper part of our fatigues and tie the sleeves around our waists. Then, as we walked between the two rows of nurses, they started giving us vaccination shots against all kinds of diseases—four shots in each arm.

From the infirmary, we went outside where a group of sergeants were waiting for us. They started calling names and directing us to fall into different groups, called flights. We finally arrived in our barracks around 0100 hours. Sgt. Elliot assigned us to our bunks and footlockers. He said lights would go off in thirty minutes and reveille would be at 0430. After the sergeant left, I remember one of the guys at the other end of the barracks saying, "Just think, we only have three years, three hundred and sixty-four days left of this." We made our bunks the best we could and went to sleep.

At 0430 hours, the bugle sounded reveille. We groaned and moaned, but the lights came on and a corporal's loud voice shouted, "Okay, you men! Are you going to sleep all day? Get dressed and fall out in five minutes!"

We all managed to get dressed and ran out in front of the barracks. After roll call, we went back into the barracks to make our beds and wash up. Then we fell out again and marched to the mess hall for breakfast. Military life had begun.

Expectation Despite the Daily Grind

Within a few days, the majority of us began to conform to the military discipline. Getting up at 0430 hours, KP duty every other week, keeping our personal items in order, and passing bed inspections every day became second nature. GI "parties" on Friday nights consisted of large buckets of water and brushes to scrub the wooden floors in the barracks. Between the eighty men in our sleeping quarters, we had ten shower stalls, ten toilets, and ten sinks. We learned to take turns and take them fast.

Marching was a daily part of life, and to add a little fun to the routine we created a chant to sing while marching: "I joined the Air Force to fly machines. What do I do? I clean latrines." It was all part of the process, though. In time, our fears and phobias about regimented life were replaced by the "esprit de corps." In three months, I had completed basic military training successfully, and most of us were promoted to the rank of private first class (airman third class today).

The next assignment was to a technical school. There were many possibilities, such as radar operator, control tower operator, radio technician, Teletype operator, drill instructor, medic, cook, firefighter, aircraft and engine mechanic, and many others. I knew I didn't want to go to cooking or fire-fighting school! My heart told me I belonged with the aircraft and engine mechanics, but I was at the mercy of the aptitude tests. When the results were announced, I had been assigned to Aircraft and Engine Mechanic School at Sheppard Air Force Base in Wichita Falls, Texas. My expectations had become reality!

I went to Sheppard Air Force Base on August 3, 1950, to undertake training as an aircraft and engine mechanic. I was assigned to a training squadron, and our group of seventeen students started aircraft and engine school. It was the typical military routine: up at 0500 hours, make our beds, wash up, march to the mess hall for breakfast, march to the flight line and to the classroom in one of the hangars, and on the first day, meet our instructor.

After a short indoctrination talk, he led us to the tool department where each student was issued a toolbox with a very good set of tools. We spent the rest of that day, and many subsequent afternoons, learning all about the use of each tool, the different sizes, and tricks of the trade. We were fortunate in having an excellent instructor, and it was obvious that he enjoyed what he was doing.

The days went by quickly as we learned about electrical, fuel, and hydraulic systems, as well as internal combustion engines, jet propulsion engines, rockets, and much more. I wasn't flying, which was still my dream, but I was becoming intimately acquainted with airplanes. I felt that in doing this work I was closer to my dream than I had ever been. I still held to the expectation that I would someday have the opportunity to continue my aviation training.

After eventually finishing the classroom phase of the course, we went out to the flight line to start applying our newly acquired knowledge on real airplanes. It was thrilling to know that we could remove an engine from one of the airplanes, take it apart, put it back together, reinstall it, make all the necessary adjustments, start it up, and it would run!

Following six months of intensive training, some of us were sent to Chanute Air Force Base in Illinois for specialized training in the maintenance of the most advanced and secret airplane of the day, the F-94B, which was the first all-weather fighter with radar and an afterburner to increase thrust. I reported to my new squadron at Chanute AFB on February 11, 1951. Training started immediately, and it proved to be as interesting as I had imagined when I first heard I had been assigned to learn all about that super-secret aircraft.

I don't think I had ever applied myself so arduously to learning anything as I did to learning all about the F-94. We were told that upon completion of the training course at Chanute

AFB, we were going to be assigned to a squadron of F-94s at Tyndall AFB, Florida. We were going to be the first group of technicians who knew anything about the F-94, and I admit that I took that responsibility very seriously.

As a result of my dedication, I graduated with the highest grade in the class. During the graduation exercises, I was given a certificate of achievement accompanied by a letter to my future squadron commander. I was also promoted to the rank of corporal. As my confidence grew and my skills in aviation mechanics increased, I felt I was coming into my own.

Normally, we were given a few days leave between assignments. However, the need for F-94 trained personnel at Tyndall AFB was urgent, so we were transported to Panama City, Florida, without delay. We were assigned to different squadrons and began working on the beautiful, new, and shiny F-94s. There wasn't much time for anything but work, as the squadrons were way behind in their flight training schedules. For the first three months, I was assigned as an assistant crew chief under Sergeant P.R. Phillips, but I was soon promoted to the position of crew chief for the following three-month period.

My greatest joy in those days was to see my airplane take off and to know that it was because of me that it was in the air. My plane flew more flight hours than any of the others, and it was always ready to go. Whenever it was due for an inspection, I would take it into the hangar after the last flight of the day and work on it most of the night, so it would be ready to go in the morning.

Sometimes, when my airplane needed a test flight, the test pilots would take me up in the radar observer's seat. I will never forget the first time I went on one of those flights, as it was my first time in a jet aircraft! When the pilot activated the afterburner, I experienced the fastest acceleration I had ever felt.

What a thrill! And it was my airplane that was doing all that, the airplane I had worked on with my own hands!

My superiors rewarded all my hard work, and I was consequently promoted, ahead of my contemporaries, to the rank of staff sergeant. At age twenty, I was one of the youngest staff sergeants in the Air Force, and I was also assigned as a flight chief in charge of twelve airplanes. Not only did I have sixteen men working under me, but I also had the reputation of surpassing all the other flights in flying time.

I was enjoying what I was doing very much, but I knew it was only a stepping-stone toward my long-awaited dream of flying. I still flew civilian airplanes occasionally at the municipal airport in Panama City. I also knew that the Aviation Cadet program in the Air Force was probably the way I could achieve my dream, but I didn't have the required education to be accepted in the program. Subsequently, I continued my education via operation "Boot Strap," which the Air Force made available to anyone who wanted to obtain a degree.

Even though my dream of becoming a pilot still seemed far away, I held tightly to the expectation that, with hard work and dedication in the present, I would see my goals come to fruition in the future. And that expectation kept my dream alive. When you live your life with expectation, you tend to look for the positive in any given situation. Even when your circumstances are tedious or trying, you know you are meant for more, and you have the expectation that you will achieve what you have set out to accomplish. When you expect to succeed, nothing can stop you. *Live your life with expectation!*

Questions

1. When the author decided to join the Air Force in order to get one step closer to his dreams, he was met with a lot of negative feedback. Have you ever felt discouraged because of lack of support for your dreams?

2. The author admits that he stopped telling just anyone about his dream of becoming a pilot because he knew that most would just shoot down his idea. Describe a time when you shared a hope or a dream with someone only to have her try to discourage you.

3. How can we learn to keep our expectations high even when everyone else around us doesn't share the same expectation? Should we only choose to be around people who are supportive? Why or why not?

4. The author shares, "My greatest joy in those days was to see my airplane take off and to know that it was because of me that it was in the air." Doing something valuable with your hands and seeing the successful result can be very fulfilling. What positive actions can you take in your own life (learn a new skill to become better at your job, create something that brings other people joy, start a building project, etc.) so that you can see a successful result?

5. The author closes this chapter by admitting that even though he was enjoying what he was doing as an aircraft mechanic, he knew it was only a stepping-stone toward his long-awaited dream of flying. How can you put your big dream in perspective (and make it less overwhelming) by creating "stepping-stones" that will get you closer to achieving your dream?

Life Lesson #9

Live Your Life with PERSEVERANCE

*"With ordinary talent and extraordinary perseverance,
all things are attainable."*

—Thomas Fowell Buxton

I worked all day and sometimes at night on the flight line, attending school whenever possible. The schedules were very flexible, making it possible for people like me to continue their education. By July 1952, I was able to pass all the tests that qualified me for the Aviation Cadet program. I was overjoyed! All of my hard work was about to pay off. My dream was becoming a reality.

However, before I could be officially assigned to the group of applicants who would be given the final acceptance tests, I had to pass the flight physical examination. It was a rigorous examination, lasting most of the morning and part of the afternoon. All the tests indicated that I was in excellent health, according to the comments of doctors and nurses. By the time I went back to my barracks, I was confident that I had passed the physical, and I would be on my way to an assignment as an aviation cadet! I couldn't sleep that night; my mind was already making plans to start another phase of my life.

I had to wait until late afternoon the following day to get the results of the physical. After waiting for what seemed like an eternity, one of the secretaries at the base hospital brought the report of my physical to me.

"You are disqualified," she said without any emotion on her face.

I could hardly believe what I was hearing and begged to know why.

"It's your eyes," she said. "Your left eye is 20/135 and the right 20/160."

Those numbers were higher than anything I had ever heard in relation to eye examinations. It didn't make any sense! I certainly didn't have any trouble seeing, but there it was, written on the form with the flight surgeon's signature under it. They even gave me a prescription for glasses.

Despite my misgivings, I trusted the doctor's report and started imagining things were wrong with my eyes. I went ahead and ordered glasses in accordance with the prescription they had given me. When the glasses came, I tried them on and things looked strange, but I rationalized that I had to get used to them. The ultimate test of the glasses was when I went to fly a light airplane at the airport in Panama City. The glasses were just not right. My depth perception was nil. I threw the glasses in the backseat and came back for another landing—then everything looked the way it was supposed to look!

After that experience, I had my eyes checked by an ophthalmologist, and they were 20/20! I went back to see the military flight surgeon and showed him the results of the eye examination by the civilian doctor; he checked my eyes again and discovered that they were 20/20. He apologized, but he said I had to wait one full year before I could reapply for the Aviation Cadet program. Those were the rules. I was certainly disappointed, but I was glad that my eyes were okay.

Learning Perseverance Through Disappointments

I worked even harder at maintaining my airplanes while I experimented with some ideas I had about how to best manage the people who worked for me. Taking on this leadership role felt like second nature. Because I was staff sergeant, these men immediately gave me the respect my rank required. We continued as the number one flight in the squadron. We flew the most hours, and our airplanes were the cleanest and sharpest on the flight line.

A year went by; as soon as it was allowed after the eye fiasco, I applied for the Aviation Cadet program again. This time I easily passed the physical and was sent to Moody Air Force Base in Valdosta, Georgia, for the final test before being assigned to a class in the program. It was an all-day test, which included psychological tests, coordination exercises, and general knowledge. It was an exhausting eight hours.

The next day I packed and got ready to return to Tyndall Air Force Base after I found out how I did on the test. All the applicants reported to the building where we had taken the test the day before. After waiting for a few minutes, a sergeant came into the room and started reading names, announcing who had qualified. When the sergeant read my name, I was shocked. I waited until he was through before I asked him why I was disqualified. He replied, "I can't tell you."

Once again I had come *this close* only to hear "disqualified." I was devastated. I didn't even wait for the bus that I was supposed to take back to Tyndall AFB. I walked out of Moody AFB and started hitchhiking. It was at times like this that the optimism my mother instilled in us got me through. I knew I would fly—just not as soon as I had hoped.

As my four-year enlistment was about to end, I opted out of reenlistment despite the promise of a ten thousand dollar reenlistment bonus and a promotion. I knew that if I persevered, I would find another way to make my dream of flying a reality.

On April 12, 1954, I was given an honorable discharge from the Air Force. With my mustering-out pay of six hundred dollars, I headed for California in a trusty 1951 Studebaker I had purchased a few months earlier.

Perseverance Through Unexpected Detours

I felt confident that I could go out and make a decent living while continuing to pursue my dream of flying. But I was soon disappointed. I could not find a job in Los Angeles. So I drove to San Diego and went directly to the employment office. When they found out about my mechanical background, they sent me to the Naval Air Station on Coronado Island, across the bay from San Diego. I reported to the employment department and was hired right away.

I was then assigned to the Overhaul and Repair department, whose function was to disassemble worn-out airplanes, refurbish or replace the worn-out parts, reassemble them, and sell the airplanes to different countries around the world. Unfortunately, it was the most boring work I have ever endured. Gone was the thrill of working on an airplane that I could see fly every day. Five minutes seemed like an hour, and a full day like an eternity. The next day was simply more unendurable boredom. The pay was okay, but not enough to enable me to continue my flight training. I had to find another job.

In my incessant search for alternate employment, I heard that Convair was expanding its operations in the Mojave Desert. I applied and was hired. It was on to my next adventure.

I reported to the Convair facility in Lancaster, California, in the Mojave Desert on January 15, 1955. The facility was part of the famous Air Force Test Pilot School and the experimental aircraft-testing field at Edwards Air Force Base in Muroc, California.

It was like looking into the future! I had never before seen such an array of aircraft as was concentrated at Edwards AFB. The majority were prototypes of models that had a fifty-fifty chance of going into production. Depending on the results of the testing at Edwards, they would either be scrapped or produced and used by the Armed Forces.

One of those prototypes was the F-102, the first supersonic fighter. I was assigned to work on this experimental model. This was much more exciting for me than working on worn-out airplanes. We made modifications and installed experimental equipment on the prototype for a couple of months. It would be ready for the test flight once we completed all the modifications.

I remember sometimes having to go to the base at 0500 hours to get the airplane ready for the flight. We would preflight it and tow it to the end of the runway. After a while, the test pilot would drive up in a pickup, dressed in his pressure suit, parachute, and helmet.

Oh, how I envied and admired him. He was willing to risk his life in an experimental machine. During the test flight, the pilot was in constant radio communication with the ground control, but we sweated every minute while he was up there at altitudes nearing the stratosphere.

Most of the test flights lasted about an hour and a half, but sometimes they had to be terminated early because of a malfunction. Happiness was when the plane flew the scheduled time and finally came down and made a perfect landing. As the airplane taxied to where we were, and the pilot shut the engine down, we knew he would have a list of things we had to modify and/or repair, so we had our work cut out for another couple of weeks or months.

I was getting paid more than I had ever made. Most important, I was able to continue my flight training. Despite the fulfillment and excitement I found working on the experimental airplanes, I continued to persevere toward my ultimate dream of becoming a pilot myself.

I started taking flying lessons at Quartz Hill Airport near Palmdale, California. The owner and chief instructor, William Pike, knew everything about aviation. He had a fleet of seven airplanes: three Aeroncas, a Tri-Pacer, a Stinson Voyager, and a couple of J-3s. He had the perfect touch, no matter which airplane he was flying, and was a great instructor.

As a result of finishing my aviation training with him, I was able to obtain my private pilot's license, and then started working toward obtaining a commercial license. Just a couple more steps in the right direction. Every step prepared me for the next one, even though I had taken some turns on my way to becoming a pilot. I knew that my perseverance had carried me through my disappointment of being disqualified from the Air Force Aviation Cadet program, the setback of having to move from Los Angeles to San Diego, the drudgery of working at the Overhaul and Repair department at the Naval Air Station, and even the distraction of the excitement of working with experimental airplanes. NOTHING could distract me from my overall goal—not failure or relative success. When you have perseverance, your life will still have challenges, but you will face them knowing that any challenge can be transformed into a stepping-stone that leads to your dream. *Live your life with perseverance!*

Questions

1. The author shared his disappointment and disbelief when he was disqualified from the Aviation Cadet program because of his eye exam. Even after he proved his 20/20 vision, he was told he had to wait a year before he could reapply. It was completely unfair. But his persistence pushed him to move on and not lose hope. Share a time when you persisted through disappointment.

2. A year after the author was disqualified from the Aviation Cadet program through no fault of his own, he reapplied, only to be disqualified again for unknown reasons. Would you have left the Air Force as the author did?

3. The author was discouraged as he left the Air Force, but he pressed on, moving to Los Angeles to find work. Even after facing discouragement at not finding work there, he moved on to San Diego. How do you deal with discouragement—do you retreat or do you press forward? Which reaction is ultimately more effective, in your opinion? Explain.

4. In his job at the Overhaul and Repair department at the Naval Air Station in San Diego, the author expressed the boredom he felt each and every day "watching the clock." He could not believe that a fellow employee wanted to stay just for a pension. How important is it to you that your job or responsibilities in life be rewarding?

5. The author felt the thrill and excitement of working on experimental new airplanes at Convair and was making more money than he ever had, but he was still set on

becoming a commercial pilot. Why should we not allow even *good* things to get in the way of achieving our goals?

Life Lesson #10

Live Your Life with AMBITION

"Intelligence without ambition is a bird without wings."

—Salvador Dali

In the process of building up my time for the commercial license, I flew the Tri-Pacer from Quartz Hill to Mexico City. The flight down was rather uneventful, but there were some anxious moments when I got low on fuel and couldn't find the airport where I had planned to land. In those days, the charts were not very accurate and the radio aids were almost non-existent. But I did manage to find the airport; I didn't go as long between refueling after that.

Making my approach into Mexico City International Airport was certainly a thrill. It had been six years since I left, not knowing how I was going to realize my dream of flying as a commercial pilot. I knew I was still a long way from achieving it, but then again, here I was, approaching the airport where I had flown for the first time in my life and where I had also flown solo for the first time. I thought it was an accomplishment of sorts, especially after just having completed a flight of one thousand five hundred miles across some of the most mountainous areas in Mexico with inaccurate charts and no electronic navigational aids.

I stayed in Mexico City five days, visiting friends and relatives and taking some of them for rides in the airplane. Then I had to return, because I had to get back to work. During my preflight check of the weather, I found out that a hurricane was heading toward Mexico City from the Gulf of Mexico. It was moving rapidly, and the weatherman recommended that I postpone my flight a couple of days. In hindsight, I should have heeded his recommendation. I barely stayed ahead of the hurricane, but I was able to return safely to Lancaster after some harrowing flying.

I continued my busy schedule working on the F-102, going to school at night, and flying every time I had a chance. I finally obtained my commercial license on April 21, 1956. I immediately started applying for a flying job, sending applications to every airline in the United States, and I applied for a position with Cessna Aircraft Company. I was sure one of them would hire me right away, but it didn't happen. I did get a letter from United Airlines, asking me to visit their employment department at Los Angeles International Airport, so I went and interviewed but was never called.

Ambition to Keep Trying

In retrospect, I should have continued applying with United and all the other airlines at least every six months, but I didn't do it. Instead, I went to an Air Force recruiting office in Lancaster and applied for the Aviation Cadet program once again. I thought I would give it one more try before I was too old (I was a year and a half shy of the maximum age). I passed all the required application tests, and seven days later I was on my way to March Air Force Base in Riverside, California, for the dreaded flight physical and the eight-hour test—the same test that had disqualified me at Moody Air Force Base in 1953.

The flight physical was as long and as thorough as the one I went through at Tyndall AFB in 1952, and it was a relief to get it over with. We were given the results of the physical before we started the daylong qualifying test the next day. I passed!

It was then on to the general knowledge tests right away. After about two hours, we started the psychological tests. We had a short lunch, and then continued on with more tests the rest of the afternoon. By 1700 hours, my brain was exhausted, but I kept answering the questions the best I could. The test administrator finally announced that we were through at 1730 hours. We had been there nine hours plus the thirty minutes for lunch.

After we were dismissed, there wasn't much to do except to wish each other luck. I drove back to Lancaster and started the long, anxious wait for the results of the test and my last attempt at being accepted into the Aviation Cadet program.

* * *

I went back to work on the F-102. We were in the middle of spin tests, and we worked on our experimental model for a whole month, getting it ready. We installed one JATO bottle under each wing tip to enable the pilot to fire one or the other to stop the spin, if he couldn't do it aerodynamically with the flight controls. We also made provisions to install a large parachute in a compartment where a smaller parachute was normally carried, to aid in deceleration after landing as a last resort.

By the time we were finally ready for the spin tests, one month had passed since my trip to March AFB. I hadn't heard anything from the Air Force, so I began to think that I had been disqualified … again. I was thankful for the intense work, day and night, to get the F-102 ready, as it made waiting for the news from the Air Force more bearable.

The day of the spin test came on a cool September day. We towed the airplane to the end of the long runway, just as the sun was coming up and the test pilot arrived in his flight suit. After powering up, the pilot gave the signal and started taxiing onto the runway. He applied maximum power and was airborne in less than fifteen seconds. Now we had to sit and "sweat." After hearing each transmission from the pilot, we got the news that the spin recovery had been achieved. Our model passed the spin test with flying colors!

Two months had passed since my return from March AFB. I went to check my post office box every day. It was always the same: bills, junk mail, and an occasional letter, but nothing from the Air Force. If I had not been the eternal optimist, I might have thought I was simply not a candidate for the Aviation Cadet program. But optimism was my impetus, so I continued going to town every day to check my mail in anticipation of that letter from the Air Force.

Meanwhile, I threw myself into my work and volunteered for everything the company wanted me to do. I had the ambition to be successful, so I continued working, flying, going to school, and dreaming.

Christmas of 1956 came, and I still hadn't heard from the Air Force. My optimism was beginning to waver. Since I had vacation time for Christmas and New Year's, I decided to take another flying trip to Mexico City. I rented the Cessna 140 from the flying club and headed south.

Pursuing the same route I had flown in the Tri-Pacer during my previous trip to Mexico City, I followed the coastline along the Pacific Ocean from Punta Peñasco, Chihuahua, all the way to Mazatlán, Sinaloa. When I landed at Mazatlán Airport and refueled, I called my Uncle Joel, who was still living in Tequila, Jalisco. I told him I was on my way to Mexico City and that I would be flying over Tequila within the next four hours. He was very excited that I was actually flying an airplane all the way from the United States. He told me about an airport in the town of Magdalena, which was located about thirty-five kilometers north of Tequila, and said he would meet me there. I gave him an ETA after I located the airport on my map and prepared to get airborne again.

The "airport" in Magdalena turned out to be nothing more than two tracks about the width of a car, totaling about one thousand feet in length. On both sides of the tracks were bushes that appeared to be about three feet tall. I circled a few more times in search of a real airport while glancing at the tracks below me. Then I decided to just go with it. I was able to land, then carefully turn the plane around, when I heard a car approaching. It was my Uncle Joel with several of his wife's relatives in the back.

It was a joyous reunion, as I hadn't seen my Uncle Joel for several years. After all the hugs and exchange of "war stories," I had to make provisions to either tie down the airplane at that dump or fly it to a real airport. But I was still out of fuel. I asked my uncle if he had any extra fuel in his car, and he replied, "Of course, how much do you need?"

"All you have," I said.

He had twenty liters, which would be enough for about forty-five minutes of flying time. I didn't like the idea of using automobile gas, but I had no choice. I checked the nearest airport on the map, and it looked as if I could make it with that fuel. We transferred the fuel, and I made plans to fly to the next airport in a town called Arenal, which was closer to Tequila.

I spent that night at my uncle's house in Tequila and left early in the morning for Mexico City. I was there for New Year's Eve 1956. It was fun being with some of my relatives and friends, but I have never been one to enjoy the drinking of alcoholic beverages, so I excused myself shortly after midnight and returned to my hotel.

As I lay awake, I reviewed what I had accomplished since leaving Mexico in 1949 in pursuit of my dream. It had been six years. I was proud of the four years I had spent in the Air Force, becoming fluent in the English language, and obtaining an intimate knowledge of airplanes. I was proud of the accomplishment of obtaining my commercial license and being able to visit with family that knew how difficult my childhood had been. Very few understood the courage and ambition it had taken to leave everything I knew to pursue my dream.

Yet I still didn't feel I was getting any closer to my dream of flying for an airline. I was almost twenty-six years old, and I was beginning to have doubts as to whether I would ever achieve that dream. If only the Air Force would accept me for the Aviation Cadet program! It sure would be a great alternative to being an airline pilot and the beginning of a wonderful future. I could just imagine being an officer and a pilot in the United States Air Force. I must have gone to sleep because I don't remember anything else, but I'm sure I must have dreamt about it. When I woke up, I felt full of optimism and was anxious to wind up my visit and head north again.

I spent a bit more time with my uncle, and then finally headed home. My first priority was to check the mail. There were piles of bills, junk mail, and a few letters, but nothing from the Air Force. Disappointed again. I was starting to get used to it.

I had one more day before I had to report to work, so I took care of all the things that had accumulated during my trip, and then returned to my job at Edwards AFB on the following day. The routine started again. Work was always interesting, and I once again lost myself in it. I continued to check the mail daily, which was no small task since I had to drive about twenty miles each way to go to the post office where I had my PO box. I was almost losing hope, and at times I considered checking the mail on a weekly basis. But I found myself still making the long drive each day, filled with optimism.

On January 20, 1957, I had had a rough day at work and really didn't feel like making the drive to town, but I did it anyway. There was only one letter in my box. It said "US Air Force, Official Business." Finally, the letter I had been waiting for—the letter that had driven me to check my mail every day in anticipation of its contents.

I couldn't open it. It could be another notification that I had been disqualified, or it could be ... I finally opened it. It was an acceptance letter! I had qualified for the Aviation Cadet program in the Air Force after all these years and two disappointing disqualifications. My ambition to continue to strive for what I wanted had finally paid off!

I almost couldn't believe it. I read and reread the letter. What a relief. I had made it! I was full of emotions. In some ways, I felt that it was bound to happen because I believed that it was my destiny. But then I thought about how close I was to the maximum age for acceptance into the program and how close I had come to not making it. I was ecstatic. I immediately filled out the form I was instructed to return to headquarters and sent it by registered mail with a return receipt.

As I waited for further instructions from the Air Force, I began getting ready for the next phase in my life. I got rid of excess baggage and cut my expenses, in order to make it on my limited cadet's pay.

On February 4, 1957, I received another letter from the Air Force with my authority for enlistment and assignment to USAF Preflight School at Lackland Air Force Base on March 5, 1957. It stated that I had met the high standards required by the United States Air Force. I was particularly focused on the words: "It is hoped that you will be successful in realizing an ambition to take your place in the United States Air Force as a rated officer."

That letter just confirmed once more that all these events taking place in my life were real. My unrelenting ambition had finally paid off with the realization of my dream to be in the Aviation Cadet program. When you live your life with ambition, you have a picture of what you want to achieve and will do the hard work to complete your vision. Ambition says no to lesser pursuits and distractions and yes to whatever it takes. *Live your life with ambition!*

Questions

1. What do you think it felt like for the author to fly into Mexico City for the first time after leaving many years before with only thirty dollars to his name?

2. He enjoyed a joyous reunion with his Uncle Joel and his family in Tequila. Do you think he ever questioned his decision to leave his uncle to pursue his dream of flying? Why or why not?

3. The author shared his experience of trying one last time to qualify for the Aviation Cadet program in the Air Force. Why do you think his ambition to fly led him back to the Air Force even after he received his commercial pilot license?

4. The author poured himself into his work on the F-102, and that work was what kept his mind off of waiting for the letter from the Air Force. What are the techniques you use to quiet your mind when you are anxiously awaiting a response?

5. The author finally received word that he had been accepted into the Aviation Cadet program. Share a time in your life when you discovered that something you had been waiting for finally came to pass.

Life Lesson #11

Live Your Life with ENDURANCE

*"Endurance is not just the ability to bear a hard thing,
but to turn it into glory."*

—William Barclay

Here I was, finally being initiated into the Aviation Cadet program in the Air Force! Only five other people were being initiated in the same cadet class. One of them was full of tales of woe; he said that only 50 percent of the students ever made it through. He spoke grimly of the chances of initiates getting through the academic program, military training, or the flying part of the training. Evidently this guy had some inside information, and you could see that he was scared of even thinking about entering such a program. Interestingly, I never saw him again. I suspect he went the route of SIE (Self-Initiated Elimination) for those cadets who didn't think they could take it.

The deployment day came, and I again packed my car with my few belongings. I realized that I was at a milestone, a threshold beyond which lay a new era in my life. It was only with incredible endurance that I had even made it to this point.

My thoughts turned to the past. I remembered my starvation days, my first flight, my days at the airport washing airplanes and helping the mechanics, my job at the Commission Against Hoof-and-Mouth Disease, and subsequently beginning a new life in the United States. I recalled the many grueling hours going to school at night to learn English and to further my education. Following this was my enlistment in the Air Force, which prompted me to excel in order that I might be in charge of the best flight in my squadron. Then there were my jobs at the Naval Air Station and finally with Convair. At long last, my future was beginning to take shape and have some real meaning. I could visualize myself as an Air Force pilot—flying fighters and eventually flying for an airline. The images in my mind were very real, and I knew now that finally it was inevitable.

My drive to Texas was probably one of the most enjoyable rides in my life, as I was convinced that my lifelong dreams were finally being realized. Arriving at Lackland Air Force Base shortly after noon on March 5, 1957, I was very sure of myself. I felt that I owned the base, since I was returning after having been promoted to the rank of staff sergeant and, better yet, as an Aviation Cadet.

That attitude was short-lived. As soon as I reported to the Cadet Squadron, the upperclassmen were waiting, and they immediately let me know my true status. The onslaught of the typical military verbal barrage began. My "tormentors" were much younger than I was and less experienced, but I knew it was their job to put pressure on us new cadets to eliminate those who couldn't take it. I could see it was going to be a long three months, but I was determined to endure. Nothing would stop me from realizing my dream. *So, come on! Dish it out. I can take whatever you have to give.*

It was late that night when the new class, 58-P, finally made it to the barracks. Basic training back in 1950 had been a picnic in comparison. Our upperclassmen were determined to break us in the first few days. They did succeed with some of my classmates who exercised the SIE privilege. But to me it was a game. Nothing, absolutely nothing, would stop me from becoming an Air Force pilot. I had my sights set on the prize, and I had to endure.

I had some difficulty with the academics portion of the program, so I wouldn't go to activities designed to give us a break, such as happy hour on Sunday afternoons. One Sunday afternoon after the rest of my flight left to enjoy happy hour at the club, I got my books out and started studying. But an upperclassman had other ideas for me. I spent the next hour opening and closing the windows to precise measurements to satisfy his whims.

Mealtime was not very enjoyable either. Seven of us cadets sat with one upperclassman. The cadets had to stand at attention until the upperclassman indicated that we could sit down. Then we had to eat "square meals," which meant that we had to raise the fork or spoon vertically from the plate to the height of our mouths, and then move the eating utensil horizontally to our mouths while sitting at attention. We never knew when the upperclassmen would say, "Mister Smith, say something intelligent." Of course, whatever we said was not intelligent enough for the upperclassman, and he would ridicule us.

I managed to make it through academics, thanks to the many hours I spent studying and an incredible amount of mental endurance. On May 31, 1957, Aviation Cadet Class 58-P graduated from preflight training. Those of us still in the program were a happy bunch. We got word that we were going to Hondo Air Base, a civilian operation about fifty miles west of San Antonio, Texas. Military personnel ran it, but the majority of the flight instructors were civilian.

We reported to Hondo Air Base the seventeenth of July— three days after my twenty-sixth birthday. It was like a country club in comparison to Lackland Air Force Base. I just had to go to the flight line the day I got to Hondo so I could drool over all those airplanes with the Air Force markings. I still couldn't believe I was soon going to start flying these machines. The following day we were issued all our flight gear: flight suits, jacket, parachute, boots, watch, sunglasses, and headset.

We were being treated like pilots already. I could hardly wait to meet my flight instructor and get started with the program. That afternoon we reported to the operations building by the flight line to meet our instructors. There were forty-nine students, of which thirty-seven were cadets and twelve were officers. We, the cadets, were going to receive our commissions upon completion of our training.

Mr. Gunstream welcomed us and gave us an outline of the primary flying course we were about to start, and then introduced us to the twenty-two flight instructors who would be working with us.

I was concerned about my prior flight experience because I had heard from some of my classmates that the Air Force preferred to teach the students the Air Force way rather than unlearning bad flying habits. I decided that I just couldn't lie about it. When Mr. Gunstream asked if anyone had previous flying experience, I raised my hand and answered with how many hours of flying time I had and what kinds of airplanes I had flown. He made some notes, and I wondered if I had done the right thing. Soon I stopped worrying, because I knew that with my desire to make it through the program I would learn the Air Force way.

After we were given our instructor assignments, we met with them individually.

"So, you have a commercial license. What kind of aircraft have you flown?" asked Mr. Brannon, my instructor.

I told him I had flown Aeroncas, Taylorcrafts, Fleets, Stearmans, Pipers, Luscombes and Cessnas and told him how many hours of flying time I had accumulated. He then asked me if I knew how to do aerobatics. I told him I had never had official aerobatic instruction but that I had taught myself to do loops, Immelmanns, split S's, spins, and Cuban eights.

"You are going to enjoy this program," he smiled and told me. "I'm sure you can solo the T-34 in a couple of hours, but regulations don't allow us to solo any student in less than eight hours."

What a joy! I was so relieved. I didn't have a worry in the world at that point. While the rest of the students were sweating about whether they could hack the program, I knew I was going to ace it. There was no doubt in my mind. I just had to continue my mindset of endurance.

We started the course the following day. Half of us went to ground school in the morning while the other half went flying, and then we switched in the afternoon. In the half that flew in the morning, I waited for Mr. Brannon to finish up with the first student while I reviewed some of the training materials. They were gone for a little over an hour for the first flight, which was called the "dollar" ride or the "free" ride. It was the only time we weren't graded.

At last, it was my turn to take my first flight in an Air Force plane, and I still marveled at the Air Force insignias painted on the wings. I got in the cockpit, fastened my parachute, seat belt, and shoulder harness. I had almost memorized the checklist, so I felt comfortable going through it in preparation to start the engine. I really felt important seeing a mechanic standing by with a fire extinguisher, giving me the signal to start the engine. I had never experienced anything like that!

The engine started after just a couple of turns of the propeller. What a great sound. What a great feeling. No matter how many times I have started an aircraft engine, it always feels as if the whole beautiful creation of aluminum, steel, Plexiglas, rubber, and fuel comes alive. All the sounds and vibrations enter into my brain through my hands on the throttle and the control stick, and I become one with the machine, a complete living entity. I had almost forgotten about Mr. Brannon sitting in the backseat, until he spoke through the intercom to tell me to give the mechanic a salute, which would indicate to him that we were ready to taxi.

"Okay, let's go see what you can do with this bird," Mr. Brannon said.

I taxied the airplane to the run-up apron next to the active runway. I turned into the wind, set the brakes, and checked the fuel selector, the propeller lever, mixture lever, the engine instruments, the propeller governor, and the ignition system. Everything checked within tolerance. I called the tower and got clearance for takeoff.

As far as I was concerned, I was by myself. I didn't hear anything from the backseat. I increased power and taxied onto the runway. As soon as the nosewheel was aligned with the runway, I advanced the throttle smoothly to full open when the airplane accelerated to sixty five knots, then I applied a little back pressure, and the airplane became airborne. Even though I had never flown an airplane with a retractable gear, I naturally reached for the gear switch and retracted the landing gear. As I was retracting the flaps, I heard a voice through my headset.

"Not bad; continue climbing and turn west," Mr. Brannon instructed. "We are going to the aerobatic training area."

It was a beautiful day with unlimited visibility. As we approached the aerobatic area, I wasn't prepared for what I saw. There must have been at least thirty airplanes practicing every kind of aerobatic maneuver you could imagine! Every airplane was either diving or going straight up, rolling, spinning, looping. It looked like a beehive. How could they keep from colliding with each other? I soon found out that you just had to become extra alert, and you gave each other room to maneuver. With the false sense of security that having an instructor in the rear seat gives you, I plunged into the melee.

"Clear the area and show me a power-off stall," Mr. Brannon ordered. I did what he asked, as he caused the airplane to enter into a spin. As the nose fell through the horizon and started to point straight down, he said, "Let it turn three times and recover heading north."

I did exactly what he wanted me to do; as I was pulling out of the dive, he told me to make a loop. I made a loop, and then he showed me the *right* way to perform a loop. I noticed that the g-forces were constant throughout his loop. He didn't have to tell me what I had done wrong. I knew that I had started my loop with an excessive amount of g's, and then I had relaxed the pull on the elevator, making my loop look oblong instead of round.

We continued practicing several other maneuvers. I would execute one, and then he would try one. By the end of the period we had performed every kind of aerobatic maneuver the T-34 was capable of doing. It was obvious that Mr. Brannon was enjoying this experience as much as I was.

As we were heading back to the base, Mr. Brannon said, "Very nice. Keep up the good work, and you won't have any trouble adapting to the Air Force ways."

I felt pride in my accomplishments so far in the Aviation Cadet program, and I looked forward to continuing to do everything I could to maintain my success. Even though I was enjoying the fruits of my endurance through the preflight training and all of the harassment, I realized that my attitude of "I will not quit" would continue to be vital to any successful venture in my life. When you live your life with endurance, you know that no matter what you face in this life, NOTHING will keep you from your goal. If you face every trial or situation with the attitude of endurance, you can achieve anything. *Live your life with endurance!*

Questions

1. When the author began the Aviation Cadet program, he was determined to get through whatever the program required of him. He had been through so much to get there that nothing could stop him. How did this attitude help him endure the rigors of the upperclassmen's tormenting?

2. The author said that he viewed the harassment of the upperclassmen as a "game" that he had to win, or endure. His strategy worked. Are there discouraging behaviors you must try to endure in your job, relationships, or life that you could view in this way in order to endure?

3. Once the author got through the Aviation Cadet preflight training, he knew that the hardest part of his Air Force training was completed. Now it was on to the "fun" part—learning to fly Air Force airplanes! But he had to learn the "Air Force way" to be successful in the program, which meant unlearning some bad flying habits. What bad habits could you try to unlearn to help you be more successful in life?

4. The author knew that the instructors were the source of what he would need to know to succeed in the Air Force. Despite the many types of instructors, the author always maintained a "teachable" attitude. How can you develop a more teachable attitude to learn from those who have already achieved a dream similar to yours?

Life Lesson #12

Live Your Life with CONFIDENCE

"With confidence, you have won before you have started."

—Marcus Garvey

I was having the time of my life. The next eight hours of flying time before I could fly solo were nothing but fun. Since Mr. Brannon wanted to accomplish something during that time besides just having fun, he started to get me ready to obtain my flight instructor rating.

As soon as I logged eight hours and one minute, August 9, 1957, I was allowed to fly solo. It wasn't as thrilling as my very first solo flight, but it was a great feeling to know that I was on my way to becoming a United States Air Force pilot. I was brimming with confidence.

On September 10, 1957, after having flown the required hours in the T-34, I transitioned into the T-28. What an airplane. It was huge in comparison to the T-34, but its flying characteristics are great, especially during aerobatics! After a few hours with Mr. Brannon showing me how to master the "beast," I felt very much at home in it.

It was great to hear reveille every morning at 0530 hours followed by the Air Force song. By 0700 hours, you could hear engines starting up at the flight line, and soon afterwards the first airplane would take off, followed by dozens of others. It was a glorious place to be in if you loved airplanes.

On October 18, 1957, I received an award certificate signed by Lt. Colonel John C. O'Donnell stating that I had been selected as "Cadet of the Month" due to my above average aptitude in military, academic, and flying phases of my training. My parents received a similar letter, and my selection was publicized in local papers and the Air Force Times. I even received an all-expense-paid weekend at a popular Texas dude ranch!

I took my final check ride in the T-28 on January 15, 1958, and after a ten-day leave, I reported to Webb Air Force Base at Big Spring, Texas, for basic training on the T-33 jet trainer. I was about to experience a type of flying that was quite different from conventional airplanes.

I took my first flight in the T-33 on February 24, 1958. I was way "behind" the airplane from takeoff to landing. Things were happening too fast for me. I completely forgot about a five-thousand-foot checklist. My instructor, First Lt. Pratt, didn't have much patience and screamed at me the entire flight. Everything was a calamity to him.

My confidence was a bit shaken, but after all, it was my first ride in a jet. After seven days of terrible weather that kept the planes grounded, I reviewed my previous flight's mistakes and thought I was going to give Lt. Pratt a good ride. Not so. He found other things he didn't like and screamed the whole hour we were flying. I finally realized he would never change his style of "instructing," so I turned him off. During the six subsequent flights, I managed to learn to fly the T-33 in spite of all the noise coming from the backseat. On March 20, 1958, I soloed the T-33. What a relief it was to fly without all the screaming.

I used my next two solo flights to get used to the airplane prior to starting formation flying. During primary training it was drummed into us to stay away from other aircraft. Now we were going to be trained to stick our airplane in a slot close enough to spit on the next plane and hold it there in clouds and turbulent air. Formation flying requires a steeling of nerves and a precision of aircraft control unknown in primary. Instruments and weather flying demand clear thinking. Formation exacts *innate reacting*. What I would learn in my training is that it's all about confidence.

The next day, I reported to the flight office thirty minutes before the briefing time to meet Lt. Schannep, my new instructor. I liked him right away. He told me he was a West Point graduate and had just finished instructor training school. My roommate and I were going to be his first students. I brought Lt. Schannep up to date as to how I felt about my proficiency in the T-33, and then he briefed me for my first formation flight.

He shared how flying formation in a jet is all about anticipating acceleration and deceleration, making constant minute adjustments to the power to maintain perfect position. Then he talked about how to join the lead airplane. He demonstrated with model airplanes as he talked. Another student and his instructor were going to take off ahead of us and would climb while circling over the field. Our task was to take off about five seconds after them and start a climbing turn in the same direction as the lead plane, but inside its turning radius. That way we would keep it in sight as we closed in to join the lead plane.

He walked us through the basics of a join up, then smiled and said, "That's the way it's supposed to happen. The most common mistake is moving in too slowly, which is natural, and you'll probably do it on your first try, but don't take all day to join in."

We talked to the other instructor and his student briefly, and then we went to our airplanes. The lead plane took off and turned; as soon as we got off the ground and retracted the gear, I started my turn to stay inside of the lead's turn. I kept an imaginary line between the lead plane and me; as we continued the climbing right turn, I got closer and closer to the lead. I was so close.

Then I started the subconscious slowing of the airplane (the old self-preservation instinct). Lt. Schannep reminded me very calmly not to reduce power at this stage of the join up. I didn't think I had reduced power, but I had. I added power, but then it was too much. Suddenly, the lead plane grew in size, and I was approaching it too fast. I felt Lt. Schannep get on the controls as we slid under and to the outside of the lead plane.

He very calmly explained the procedure again. By this time, I was completely soaked in perspiration. I took the controls and started the join up again. This time I closed in rather slowly again, but I managed to come up to the lead and get in the right slot. I was having a little trouble keeping the airplane from bobbing up and down, but after a few minutes, I settled down and Lt. Schannep called the lead and told him he could start making a few turns. He told me to keep the plane in position no matter what the lead plane did.

The lead plane started a gentle turn to the right; I hung in there, my eyes riveted to where the wing of the lead plane joined the fuselage. As I was congratulating myself for the perfect position I was keeping, the lead plane started a turn to the left, which sent my brain into overload, and I lost it. Suddenly, I was bobbing up and down. I peeled off to the right to put as much distance between the two planes as possible. This was much harder than I thought it was going to be.

"I've got it," Lt. Schannep said. I took my hands off the controls as he said, "Just relax and let me demonstrate what we are trying to do."

He proceeded to execute a perfect join up, and then maneuvered with the moves of the lead plane as if we were welded to it. No matter what the lead plane did, we were right there a few inches off his right wing. After a few turns, Lt. Schannep told me to get my hands on the controls and follow him through. Then he told the lead plane instructor to make a barrel roll. We stayed with him all through the roll. It was beautiful! After the barrel roll, he told the instructor to continue making gentle turns to the right and to the left. Then he said to me, "You've got the plane."

That demonstration was what my brain needed. I was still a little rough on the controls, but I managed to stay in the right slot no matter what the lead plane did.

We continued practicing the join-up maneuver and formation flying for three hours. I began to relax as we headed back to the base. The movement of my hands on the controls and the throttle became surer, and we were one with the lead plane. We flew in formation all the way to the base, and even entered the traffic pattern in formation. I started my turn to base as I lowered the flaps; we came in for a perfect landing as the lead plane was taxiing off the runway. We parked the airplane and shut down the engine.

"Well, what do you think about formation flying?" Lt. Schannep asked while we were waiting for the mechanic to bring us the ladder to get down. I told him I was amazed that I had been able to do it.

"When I fell out of formation after the first attempt, I had the terrifying thought that I might not have what it takes to fly formation," I said.

"Don't feel like the Lone Ranger," he said. "I think we all feel that way during our first attempt at formation flying. You just have to do what you did: get back in there and prove to yourself you can do it. Some students give up right then and there and decide that this kind of flying is not for them, and they SIE."

It truly was all about confidence.

The mechanic was hanging the ladder from the cockpit rail by then. Lt. Schannep started to get down and I followed him. The mechanic gave me a smile when he saw my perspiration-soaked flight suit.

Now that I had had a taste of formation flying, everything made a lot more sense as we debriefed. I knew that if I kept at it, I would continually grow in confidence in the skills required of formation flying. Lt. Schannep said we would alternate with other students leading and flying wing for a couple of days, then we would start formation takeoffs, and eventually, we would start four-aircraft formation training, night formation, and finally formation aerobatics.

From that date in March 1958 until graduation in July 1958, it was nothing but hard work and feelings of inadequacy mixed with feelings of triumph. The time went by quickly. We alternated flying with ground school. In addition to formation flying, we were spending a lot of time learning more about instrument flying, night flying, and navigation. In ground school, we were learning more about the function of our bodies when we leave our natural environment. We had to prepare ourselves to experience g-forces, blackouts, grayouts, and how to jettison and bail out of a crippled airplane.

As we were approaching graduation day, we had turned into very confident formation pilots. The only hurdle left was the dreaded instrument check. We were expected to demonstrate to a check pilot that we were capable of flying from takeoff to landing strictly by the use of instruments, all while flying from the backseat under a hood. The check pilot would sit in front and serve as safety pilot.

My 60-4 check was scheduled for June 13, 1958. Capt. Paul Leming, director of military training, was assigned as my check pilot. I felt very confident after the many hours Lt. Schannep and I had spent practicing instrument flying. However, there was that element of doubt as to whether I could perform all the requirements of the check in a satisfactory manner. Failure of this check could wash a student out of the program. This was serious business.

I reported to Capt. Leming's office at 0700 hours, and he was ready and waiting for me. He told me to sit down, and then proceeded to brief me about the check. After the briefing he asked if I had any questions, but I just wanted to get out and do it!

We preflighted the airplane and got into our seats. As he started the engine, I organized my charts and maps on my clipboard.

"Your airplane," he said after he taxied onto the runway centerline.

I checked the heading indicator once more to make sure it was indicating runway heading as I added power and released the brakes. The 60-4 check had begun. Everything seemed to go smoothly.

"That was great flying," Capt. Leming said as we were flying back to Webb AFB. "I don't know if you will ever again fly as well as you just did."

After we landed and parked the airplane, we went to Capt. Leming's office, and he told me I had passed the check with flying colors. All the apprehension I had felt before takeoff had left me as soon as we got airborne. It was as if we were on rails. My control of the aircraft was perfect. All the air maneuvers were right on the money, and according to Capt. Leming my approaches were outstanding. What a great feeling! As I walked out of his office, I finally knew I was going to graduate and get my wings and second lieutenant bars.

Before we knew it, it was July 23, 1958—one of the most memorable days in my life. It was graduation day for Aviation Cadet Class 59-A, and I was one of the graduating cadets. I had made it! My mother, my sister Dora, and my girlfriend, Joyce, were all able to attend my graduation.

Daylong festivities for the graduating cadets and their guests led up to the culmination of the day—the graduation ceremony.

The forty-two graduating cadets marched in, dressed in their Class A uniforms, with cadet shoulder boards. I glanced to the left and saw my mother, sister, and Joyce, and I gave them my biggest smile.

As soon as we were seated, the chaplain started the ceremony with a prayer. After the base commander and two other speakers were featured, something surprising happened. The training officer walked to the microphone.

"Second Lieutenant Donald J. Smith, please come forward," he said.

I was stunned. I wondered why I was being called ahead of everyone else. I got up, looked at my mother, and walked to the front. I shook hands with the training officer.

He gave me my wings and second lieutenant bars, and then he read a document he was holding that said that I had been designated a Distinguished Graduate of the United States Air Force Pilot Training. What an honor! He shook my hand again, continuing to say that I had demonstrated the ability, initiative, and other leadership qualities so essential to successful performance of duty as an Air Force officer. Then he congratulated me on my outstanding achievement.

I honestly don't recall much about the rest of the ceremony. I was overwhelmed. The next thing I knew was that my mother, Dora, and Joyce were pinning my wings, taking off the cadet shoulder boards, and pinning my second lieutenant bars. I was living my dream!

I always knew that I had the ability and initiative to complete the Air Force Aviation Program, but I had excelled to the point that I was recognized above my peers for my outstanding achievement. What I had seen as just hard work and determination was recognized as exceptional. I had the confidence to conquer each phase of the learning process, from formation flying to aerobatics, and that confidence was crucial to the highly demanding flying techniques we learned. Whatever obstacles or challenges you face in your life, have the confidence that you can overcome them. When you live with confidence, you won't let anything stand in the way of your dreams. *Live your life with confidence!*

Questions

1. During an intense part of the author's training, he had to "turn off" the screaming of his instructor and trust that he knew what it took to learn. He went through the maneuvers that were expected of him, and he didn't let his confidence dip because of one discouraging instructor experience. Are there times when you had to "turn off" negative feedback from others to maintain confidence in yourself?

2. When learning formation flying, the author had to override his "self-preservation" instinct to slow down when attempting to join up with the other jet. Can you think of any self-preservation techniques you use in your own life that could be holding you back (procrastination, withdrawal from others, not taking chances, etc.)?

3. The instrument flying check was a big obstacle to overcome for all of the pilots. The author approached it with confidence and just wanted to "get it done." As a result, he was calm and relied on his instincts and flying skill and ended up passing the flight check with flying colors. When you are faced with a test, are you more prone to feel apprehension or excitement, and how do you think that affects your performance? Explain.

4. The author was finally living the dream of being an Air Force pilot, and he was able to enjoy the reward of the final graduation ceremony. He was even given a special honor of being designated a distinguished graduate. The whole experience gave him even more confidence that he was doing what he was meant to do in life. What accomplishments can you celebrate right now that can add confidence to your ability to achieve your overall goals?

Life Lesson #13

Live Your Life with ENTHUSIASM

"Success is the result of going from failure to failure without losing your enthusiasm."

—Winston Churchill

After a twenty-day leave, I reported to Williams Air Force Base at Chandler, Arizona. As a distinguished graduate from pilot training, I had been given my choice of airplane for advanced training. That would determine the type of airplane I would be flying once I was assigned to an operational squadron. I knew without a doubt the plane that I wanted—the F-86F. It was, at the time, the best fighter in the inventory. Who wouldn't approach such an amazing airplane with enthusiasm? It was incredible.

I will never forget my first flight in the F-86. I had already learned all about its systems, so I was very familiar with it. We taxied out from the flight line in formation and took off.

The F-86 had almost double the power of the T-33. I felt like I was in a rocket! It flew beautifully. If I hadn't been "glued" to the instructor's airplane, I know I would have exceeded the maximum speed allowed in the traffic pattern, but by flying in perfect formation with him, we all kept our speed within the allowed parameters.

We climbed to twenty-five thousand feet and did some acrobatics in formation to get used to the airplane; then we headed to an auxiliary field to shoot landings. We alternated touch-and-go landings, and every landing was a "grease job" (super smooth).

What a delight! By the third landing, I felt like I had been flying the F-86 all my life.

By the time we got back to Williams AFB, we came in formation and shot an overhead approach, lining ourselves up behind the instructor in a three-plane formation. The instructor pitched his airplane into a 90-bank turn as he reduced power to idle. We followed suit and landed one after another like pros.

That was just the beginning of nothing but unadulterated fun for the next four months. We were involved with air combat maneuvers (ACM), air-to-air gunnery, dive-bombing, rocket launching, special weapon delivery, and a lot of formation flying.

On November 7, 1958, the operations officer announced that the local authorities had given permission to practice supersonic maneuvers. We had been waiting several days for this opportunity, not knowing if it would ever be granted, since the sound can be very disturbing to surrounding residents. When it was my turn to break the sound barrier, I didn't hear the sonic boom, because it is projected way ahead of the airplane, but I did feel it. It was incredible! The sound barrier had been broken for the first time only twelve years earlier, and here I was, nine years after I had arrived in the United States, flying an Air Force fighter faster than the speed of sound. If that isn't living a dream, I don't know what is.

As the program was coming to an end, we were put on orders to go to Nellis AFB near Las Vegas, Nevada, to be checked out on the F-100, a step up from the F-86. That sounded great. It was also logical, since the reason we had chosen the F-86 was to be assigned to a fighter squadron when we completed all our training.

When Enthusiasm Is Tested

That's when I learned about the "needs of the service." Just as we were clearing the base to head to Nellis AFB, six of us were called to headquarters where we were given orders to go to Stead AFB for survival training, and then to McConnell AFB for B-47 training. We couldn't believe it! It was like a slap in the face. Here we were, fighter pilots, and we were being sent to fly bombers. I was sure I would get out of this somehow, and the other five guys felt the same way. Once you are assigned to the Strategic Air Command (SAC), however, you are in for the duration. I felt deflated.

At the same time I was given the bad news about going to the Strategic Air Command, I was also about to follow through with the commitment I had made to the young lady who had been at my graduation, Joyce. We had continued to date after graduation and saw each other a couple of times while I was going through the F-86 training. I began to think that she was the woman with whom I would share my life. I asked her to marry me when I finished my training at Williams.

SAC is definitely not the type of duty conducive to success in married life. I worried about my ability to give my new wife the time and attention she deserved. But after working so hard to achieve my flying dreams, and at twenty-seven years old, I found myself saying, "Will you marry me?"

Joyce and I were married in Big Spring, Texas. We had a short honeymoon in Guadalajara, Mexico, and then I returned to El Paso to continue my Air Force career as a married man.

My orders were to report to Stead Air Force Base at Reno, Nevada, in February 1959, for survival training, then McConnell Air Force Base in Wichita, Kansas, in March 1959, for the academic portion of B-47 training. Lastly, I was to report to Little Rock Air Force Base for the flying portion of the B-47.

It was most disappointing, but there was not much I could do. My choices were to go through the B-47 training and be miserable, or find the positive aspect of this turn of events, get as much out of it as I could, and enjoy the new challenge, which has always been my modus operandi. I chose to live with enthusiasm, no matter the challenge.

And it was a challenge. Everything was a challenge in the Strategic Air Command, and for a good reason. Their motto tells the story: "Peace Is Our Profession." It was the Strategic Air Command, with its strict discipline, its grueling training exercises, and its formidable fleet of bombers that maintained air superiority over Russia during the Cold War.

So I did my part. I learned to fly the six-engine bomber and its strategic function. Our training missions would last from nine to twelve hours, and typically we would fly from four thousand five hundred to six thousand miles during that time. Each training flight was packed with different exercises such as air refueling, celestial navigation, bombing runs, air gunnery against "enemy fighters," low-level navigation, and bombing techniques. We were so busy going from one exercise to the other that we often didn't have time to eat our box lunches. But that's what you do when you want to be the best. And we were the best!

We reported to Little Rock AFB on June 10, 1959, to begin flight training in the six-engine B-47 built by Boeing. The first order of business was discovering crew assignments. Up until this time, I was the only "crew" in any airplane I ever flew. Now I was going to be one of a crew of three. There would be an aircraft commander, a navigator, and I was going to be the co-pilot. The idea of losing my independence as a fighter pilot, and then having to be part of a crew was probably the hardest part of this transition.

On the other hand, I ultimately wanted to be a commercial pilot, so I decided to look at it from that point of view. I threw myself into the arduous training, and by September 3, 1959, we finished as one of the best crews in our class. We were ready to go and be a productive part of the Strategic Air Command and were assigned to Hunter AFB in Savannah, Georgia.

I packed up my little family, and we prepared for the move. My wife had given birth to our first child, a little girl, on August 8, so I now had much more to pack. Being a father was another new training that I wish had come with a manual. I loved my baby, Yolanda, though, and like flying, found this training to be pure joy. I approached the love and care of my baby with the same enthusiasm that I embraced in my career.

After a few travel and settling-in days, I finally reported to my first operational squadron, and my life as a SAC pilot began. The majority of the missions we flew were classified as secret. I was privileged to have a top-secret clearance at that time, and I wouldn't have divulged any information connected with those missions to anybody.

When I joined the Air Force the second time, it was with the intention of making it a career. However, with all the time away from home, I realized that SAC would not allow me the time I needed with my family. In July 1962, between the Berlin crisis and the Cuban crisis, I submitted my letter of resignation, which was accepted in October 1962. In a matter of two weeks after I received my discharge, I was a civilian again.

This part of my life and training required an unyielding enthusiasm in me that I had cultivated throughout my entire life. In times that were exciting and rewarding, such as training on the F-86F, I had an understandable enthusiasm for my work. But even when I was challenged or disappointed, as I was initially when assigned to SAC, I still chose to have an enthusiasm for the work. Yes, flying bombers was not my first choice, but I made a decision to see the positive side of working with a crew and doing something meaningful and significant for my country. When you live with enthusiasm, you realize that you have a choice to maintain a positive attitude as you navigate your way through life's challenges. Choose to be positive. *Live your life with enthusiasm!*

Questions

1. The author had pride in his accomplishments and was thrilled to be assigned to the F-86F, one of the most advanced fighter jets of the time, for training. His enthusiasm for life and all the hard work that had led up to this point was paying off. Do you think an attitude of enthusiasm would have the same effect on achieving your goals?

2. The author shares his disappointment when he is assigned to the Strategic Air Command to fly the B-47 bomber. He wanted to be a fighter pilot, but he knew he had to follow orders. Even in the midst of that disappointment, he found enthusiasm for his work. What attitude would you have had if you were in his situation?

3. The author married his sweetheart, Joyce, amidst all of the upheaval in the Air Force. As he had to begin thinking of his family in addition to his own needs, he realized that the Air Force might not be the best place for him. Have you ever had to make a decision that affected not just you but someone you loved as well? Explain.

4. What areas of your life could use a little more enthusiasm? Could you be more of a positive influence at work or at home? Could you approach volunteer obligations or even the tedium of errands with the thought that you can make a difference in someone's life? Share your ideas.

Life Lesson #14

Live Your Life with PATIENCE

"If patience is worth anything, it must endure to the end of time. And a living faith will last in the midst of the blackest storm."

—Mahatma Gandhi

I was thirty-one years old, just discharged from the Air Force, and I was not quite ready for civilian life. To make matters worse, the airlines would not hire a pilot older than twenty-nine. I hadn't researched the job market for other occupations, and I had a wife and two children to support. Almost three years after having our first daughter, my wife gave birth to Rhonda while we were living in Savannah. It was not the most ideal time to be making such a change in my career, and I was concerned about how I would support my family. I was crazy about my two little girls and wanted to give them the world.

The one plan I had at the time was to take Joyce and the girls to stay with her parents in Lubbock, Texas. Then I planned to join an Air National Guard squadron nearby that would allow me to find a job or start some kind of business. Being in the Air National Guard would make it possible for me to continue flying, and it would provide a small income. My business idea revolved around buying and selling used aircraft.

We stored our furniture and headed to Lubbock in a little Renault automobile. I left my family with my in-laws and ended up in Phoenix, Arizona, where the Air National Guard had a squadron of F-104s. I was certain it would be difficult to get into that outfit, because the F-104 was one of the most sophisticated fighters in the Air Force inventory; but, to my surprise, they had a slot for a first lieutenant. I signed up and began transition training immediately.

A member of the Air National Guard has to serve a minimum of one weekend per month, which is considered four drills, and two weeks of active duty in the summer. Since transition training is a full-time job, I was, for all practical purposes, fully employed for at least a couple of months. I started ground school to learn to fly the F-104, and also started looking for a civilian occupation for when my guard pay would be reduced to the four drills per month.

I learned right away that Phoenix was not the place for my one idea of a used aircraft business. The great majority of people with discretionary income were retired, with no desire to buy airplanes or even learn to fly. I realized that I had chosen the worst possible place to try to make a go of things. In the meantime, I was getting letters from Lubbock that the situation there was rather tense, which was to be expected. The only bright outlook was my involvement with the Air National Guard and the prospect of flying the hottest fighter available at that time.

To bring relief to my family, I rented a house that I could afford under the circumstances. It wasn't a great looking house, but it served our purposes. Joyce and the girls came to Phoenix to a sparsely furnished home, but we were together.

Patience When Things Don't Go Right

I had another big letdown once again in my flying career. Just before I started the flying portion of the F-104 training, it was announced that C-97s were immediately replacing the F-104s. The C-97 was a big, lumbering thing that was designed as a cargo plane. In the aviation circles it is said that the C-97 has a calendar instead of an air speed indicator. It was that slow. My patience began to wear thin.

What else could go wrong? It was almost like those times in Mexico when all the doors closed on me. I needed a dose of my mother's optimism. If I hadn't had that optimism, I'm sure I would have succumbed to the belief that what I was experiencing was a result of bad choices on my part. What I needed was to believe that I could get back on track.

Many of the members of my squadron moved to Tucson where they could fly F-100s. I wasn't in a position to do that because of my financial situation, so I stayed and started training in the C-97.

Meanwhile, I kept looking for a civilian job. After a short stint trying to sell insurance, I saw an ad in the paper from the Phoenix Police Department recruiting patrolmen. I was getting desperate by then, so I went and applied. I went through all the testing and physical examinations and finally was called to appear before the hiring board. A large table held six police officers: a captain, two lieutenants, and three sergeants. They told me to sit down and started asking questions. After about twenty-five minutes, which seemed like an eternity, the captain said, "Why do you want to be a policeman?"

"To begin with, I need a job," I said. "As you know, I have been in the service of our country for the last nine years. Flying is my profession, but we are going through a cycle in the aviation business when there is very little hiring, or none at all. I thought I would seek employment in another service organization until I'm able to get back in the flying world."

"How long do you think it will take for you to get a job flying?" he asked.

"It could be one month, or a couple of years," I told him.

"I really don't think you are the kind of person we want as a police officer," the captain said.

"I have to respect your opinion, because you know what the job requires," I said. "And after all your questions, you know me very well. Thank you for considering me anyway."

I started to get up to leave the room.

"Sit down," the captain said, holding up his hand. "You are hired, if you want the job."

I was surprised, after what he had just said. He explained that they always told applicants that they didn't think they were the kind of person they wanted as police officers to see their reaction. He said that how the applicant reacted gave the hiring board another measure of each individual's real motives for wanting to serve in the police department.

Once again, I started another adventure in my life.

I was glad to have the job because it meant I could take care of my family, but the thought crossed my mind that I might wind up doing police work the rest of my working years. What about my flying dreams? I had sent applications to airlines all over the world, aircraft manufacturers, the Federal Aviation Administration (FAA), and air ambulance organizations. I had even applied for jobs as an aircraft mechanic, thinking I might wind up getting connected in the aviation business and eventually get a flying job. But none of the applications had brought any results.

It was December 15, 1962, when I started as a new recruit in the Phoenix Police Academy. I put all the concerns I had out of my mind, and I did what I always do when I'm faced with a learning task. With a truckload of patience, I threw myself into it and tried to do my best. It turned out to be a very interesting three months. The instructors were veterans who had seen everything in law enforcement. We learned early on that we were going to be making life-and-death decisions as soon as we were assigned to our beats.

The next three months were packed with rigorous physical training every day, getting familiar with our weapons, learning all about the laws of arrest and seizure, civil and criminal law, traffic management, and many other subjects related to law enforcement and serving the public. We also spent many hours at the shooting range. As a result of all this training, I was in the best physical condition I have ever been in, and I was an expert in the use of a handgun.

I graduated from the Phoenix Police Academy as a patrolman on March 15, 1963, and was assigned immediately to the southeast part of the city. My hopes of being hired by one of the many flying organizations were slowly fading, but I was proud to be a member of the Phoenix Police Department. They were a group of very dedicated individuals. As a rookie, I was assigned to work with some of the old-timers who were always willing to teach me the ropes.

It turned out to be very fascinating work, but I didn't want to spend much time away from the flying world. Of course, I was able to continue flying the C-97s in the Air National Guard, but my plan was to fly for a commercial airline, if at all possible.

I soon adapted to police work, but kept anxiously checking my mail every day. It was like the days when I was waiting for my letter of acceptance for the Aviation Cadet program, and just as frustrating when weeks went by without any response to the many applications I had sent.

Several months after I had been assigned to my beat, when I was beginning to think I was going to be in law enforcement the rest of my working life, I received three offers the same day. One was from the FAA offering me a position as a navigation facilities inspector, where I would be flying various types of aircraft and checking the accuracy of navigation facilities. The second offer was from Eastern Airlines for a flight engineer position.

The third offer was from Cessna Aircraft Company, who was looking for a regional service manager. The job would entail being assigned an aircraft and covering a region as a factory service representative. This position required a commercial license with an instrument rating and a minimum of one thousand two hundred hours flying time as well as an aircraft and engine mechanic's license and the ability to speak Spanish fluently. The position seemed to be perfectly designed for me since I easily met all the requirements.

Talk about feast or famine! One day I was losing hope that I would ever get back in the flying game, and the next I had to decide between three offers! I got in touch with Cessna, Eastern Airlines, and the FAA and set up appointments for interviews.

I set up an interview with Eastern Airlines in Los Angeles. When I called Cessna I was told that the service department manager was planning to be in Phoenix the following day, and that he was willing to come to my house to meet me and my wife. I was impressed, and a little apprehensive, at the prospect of having a VIP coming to my rather modest home, but I told his secretary that I would be expecting him. The FAA gave me a date in the future for an interview.

The following day, I got home around eight in the morning after working all night patrolling the streets of southeast Phoenix. I helped Joyce straighten up the house, took a shower, and waited for Mr. Kangas, Cessna's worldwide service manager. I didn't have to wait long. At 10:00 a.m. sharp, we heard a car outside and then heard a knock on the door.

Wearing a dark suit and eyeglasses, Mr. Kangas was about fifty-five years old and about six feet tall. He had a warm smile when he introduced himself to Joyce and me. He took a few minutes to talk to the girls before he said down.

"You mentioned in your application that you are working for the Phoenix Police Department. Why aren't you flying?" he asked.

I pointed to the room where the girls had gone and told Mr. Kangas that my primary concern was to provide for them. Then I showed him the file with all the copies of applications I had sent to organizations in the aviation field. I also mentioned to him that I was a member of the Air National Guard and that I was in the process of being trained in the C-97 to fly missions in the United States, Asia, Europe, and South America.

Mr. Kangas then asked me if I had experience in light airplanes. I gave him a synopsis of my flying career, which included my flying time in light aircraft such as Cessnas, Pipers, Taylorcrafts, Stinsons and Aeroncas, as well as all the aircraft I had flown in the Air Force, and presently, in the Air National Guard. He wanted to see my logbooks, which I had ready for him. He seemed impressed.

He told me that Cessna Aircraft Company was looking for a person with my qualifications for the position of regional service manager. He asked me if I would be able and willing to travel anywhere in the world. He mentioned that a typical schedule for a domestic assignment was one week out in the assigned territory and one week home. For international assignments, it would be two weeks out and one week home. I would be assigned a personal airplane to cover my territory, and my job would be to visit the distributors, their dealers, and occasionally some of the customers. As a factory representative, I would have to make sure that both the distributors and dealers had a properly stocked parts department and the personnel to support their dealers' maintenance departments.

Mr. Kangas took a lot of notes and told me I would be hearing from them. He called a taxi and we exchanged a few more questions before it was time for him to leave.

It all sounded like a dream assignment to me, especially at that time when I thought my chances of getting back into the aviation field were getting very slim. Had I not had the patience to wait out the twists and turns in my career journey, I would have missed out on this amazing opportunity. Had I never been an airplane mechanic or learned to speak English or taken the time to obtain my commercial license, I would not have been suited for the job with Cessna. But as it often goes in life, each step (and misstep) often adds up to the whole of your experience that eventually leads to your dream. Even when life does not go your way, or you have to take a detour on the way to your dream, never give up. When you live with patience, you know that sometimes you must work slowly toward your dream. You never know when a new opportunity will present itself. *Live life with patience!*

Questions

1. While the author was challenged to adjust to civilian life, he started sending out applications for a flying job in any area of aviation that was available. What practical steps can you take to move toward your dream, even if it doesn't get you all the way there?

2. When flying jobs were not working out for him, the author joined the local Air National Guard to provide some kind of income and have the opportunity to fly a fighter jet, the F-104. Even though it was not a commercial airline, it was still a step in the right direction in his mind. Do you think the author regretted his decision to resign from the Air Force at this time? Why or why not?

3. Without any other prospects, the author did what he had to do to provide for his family and took the steps to become a police officer in Phoenix. Although it was far removed from his desired field of aviation, he patiently waited for an opportunity to fly again and learned a lot in the process. What can you learn in your situation right now to make it a worthwhile part of the journey to your dream?

4. After waiting patiently for months, the author finally received three different offers for employment in aviation. Have you experienced this kind of "feast or famine" in your life? Explain.

Life Lesson #15

Live Your Life with SERVICE

"Only a life lived for others is the life worthwhile."

—Albert Einstein

My mind reeled with the possibilities presented to me, especially after having limited options for so long. After briefly accepting the job as a flight engineer with Eastern Airlines, I decided to pursue the job as regional service manager with Cessna, since it would allow me to continue flying and would offer more interesting work. Leaving the Phoenix Police Department was a bittersweet experience, although I was excited to take on a new challenge. I had met many dedicated police officers who took me under their wing and taught me a lot about police work and serving the public, and in the process they had become good friends.

Our family headed for Wichita, Kansas. It was Thursday, May 2, 1963. Yolanda was almost four years old, and Rhonda was going to turn one the following month. Rhonda had turned out to have my olive complexion and deep brown eyes. She had a mischievous sparkle in her eyes, and she loved to follow her big sister in whatever she was doing. Car rides were still big adventures for the little ones. We arrived in Wichita on Saturday. I found a motel near the Cessna factory and got some needed rest after putting the girls to bed.

We found a house to rent near the Cessna plant, and I reported to Mr. Kangas on the following Monday. He had quite the itinerary for me. I met the personnel in the service department office, a couple of the other regional service managers who happened to be in town, and my secretary, Mary Ann Beamon. We then toured the assembly line where the different Cessna models were being built, the aircraft delivery center, and Cessna's military assembly line.

There I met quite a few of the engineers responsible for designing and modifying all the models being built in that plant. Everyone was very busy, but as we approached the different stations, each one greeted me with enthusiasm. I found out later that there was mutual admiration between the engineering department and the regional service managers. We were their eyes and ears out in the field as well as the first line of contact with the distributors, dealers, and customers. Many of the modifications were made as a result of what we found in our role as "test pilots" and in our contacts with the customers. I was beginning to see this as a very enjoyable career choice.

I got checked out on all of the Cessna models and continued my training at the Cessna facility along with members of the Cessna dealerships from all over the world. I was assigned to attend these classes so I could learn all about every airplane in the Cessna line. My mechanical background came in handy, and I began meeting many people with whom I would be working out in the field.

I was assigned to go out on my first trip in June 1963, with Jay McCleod, the regional service manager for the Southeast region. We would be visiting some distributors and their dealers in that region, and Jay would be showing me the ropes. I had spent some time with Jay before our trip, going over the status of the distributorships, dealerships, and customers we were going to visit and the purpose for each trip. I carefully observed him and took notes throughout the trip. I could see I had a lot to learn, but I was up for it, especially since we were talking about airplanes!

My next trip was with another regional service manager, Paul Addison, who covered the Northwest United States. By then I was doing most of the presentations to the dealers and handling some warranty cases directly with the customers. I loved every minute of it. I loved the feeling of serving others and making sure that their needs were met.

Right when I began to find my stride with Cessna, Mr. Gartin (Gart) replaced Mr. Kangas. He called me in one day to let me know I would be replacing Paul Addison as the regional service manager to the Northwest region. He told me to let the delivery center know that I needed an airplane and to let them know what model I wanted, what color, and how much equipment.

I received my airplane in September 1963 and left on my first "solo" assignment the following day. I visited distributors and dealers all across the Northwest; it was challenging but rewarding work. Ultimately customer satisfaction was everybody's goal. I did my best to assist both the company and those in my region that I served.

Eventually I was assigned to cover the entire region west of the Rockies, from Alaska to Mexico. I had nine distributorships and one hundred ten dealerships. I scheduled visits to each distributor and their dealers at least every three months. When Cessna decided to de-centralize into five regions, I was pleasantly surprised when I was notified that Tony Lansbarkis and I had been selected to go to San Francisco as the regional sales and service managers for the Western region. We met in San Francisco to look for office space, hire a secretary, and get the necessary furniture and equipment. We also had to find an airport to park and maintain our fleet of six airplanes. We made all the arrangements to start operations and move our families as soon as possible.

Just about the time we were going to start the move to the West Coast, Cessna received an order from the Peruvian Air Force for twelve 411s, contingent on their inspection of the airplane. They were in need of fifty airplanes, but they wanted to start with twelve and order the remaining thirty-eight over the following three years. This would be a very big sale for Cessna!

Sales and Service Go Hand in Hand

On March 27, 1965, Gart called me into his office and told me a 411 was on an introductory tour of Central and South America. The airplane would eventually be delivered to a customer in Montevideo, Uruguay. Ralph Matos, the sales manager for South America, was demonstrating it to all the dealers along the way. Gart wanted me to join Ralph to assist in the demonstration of the 411 to the Peruvian Air Force pilots.

I met Ralph in Panama City, where he briefed me on his flight plans and all the stops along the way. The culmination of the trip would be the big demonstration in Lima, Peru, for the Peruvian Air Force. We were very confident that the order for the first twelve airplanes would be in our hands once they had the opportunity to fly the machine. We would visit a few other South American customers, distributors, and dealers after the demonstration, but we knew the importance of the stop in Peru.

After our initial stops, we were finally going to do what we had been sent to do—meet with the Peruvian Air Force for their substantial, potential order. On Thursday, April 1, we went to the Peruvian Air Force headquarters and met with the evaluation team of six officers. They expressed their desired itinerary for the demonstration, which was to fly to an air force base near Cuzco, Peru, shoot a series of landings on the unpaved runway, and return to Lima. That meant flying across the western range of the Andes at an altitude of twenty-six thousand feet to test the airplane's high altitude performance at its maximum gross weight.

Ralph and I spent that afternoon planning the next day's flight. We checked all the performance charts, drew the course on the map, and got familiar with the few airports that were available in case of an emergency along the flight route. We felt like we were quite prepared for the demonstration and fairly confident of the impending sale.

At 0700 hours on the morning of the big demonstration, Ralph and I started the preflight check to be ready for an 0830 departure. It looked like we would have to make an instrument takeoff and departure due to the ever-present fog at the Lima airport.

The Peruvian Air Force pilots arrived at 0800 hours; they also wanted to check the airplane. When they were satisfied the airplane was airworthy, we all climbed aboard. Ralph got in the left seat, the major in the right seat, and the other five officers and myself in the passenger seats. It was time to show them what the Cessna 411 offered.

Once we were through the fog, the weather was clear with unlimited visibility. The major increased the rate of climb and turned east toward the Andes. I could see that they all were very impressed with the performance. As we were approaching the mountains, it was obvious that we were going to clear them with no problem. We all donned our oxygen masks. I was sure that Ralph and I were thinking the same thing: *We have it made! This is one awesome machine. There is no way any pilot worth his salt wouldn't fall in love with it.*

As I was basking in my thoughts, my ears picked up an undesirable sound accompanied by an out of synchronization rumble. This was an indication that the two engines were out of sync, but it was more of a nuisance than a problem, since the pilot could manually sync the engines if the automatic synchronization failed. But I didn't like it, especially not in a demonstration flight.

And then the unthinkable happened. What I was hearing was a precursor to a failure of one or both of the wastegate automatic controllers, which maintained a constant manifold pressure through the turbochargers to the engines, regardless of altitude. More than likely one had failed, and when the RPMs started to fluctuate, the automatic synchronization system caused a fluctuation of the opposite engine as well.

The tachometers were going wild, increasing and decreasing RPMs. We were just passing through eighteen thousand feet; there was no way we could continue our flight to the air force base near Cuzco, because there was still higher terrain ahead of us. This did not look good.

Ralph took the controls, reduced power on both engines, and turned 180 degrees to return to Lima. Talking through the intercom, he announced to all of us what I'm sure the Peruvian pilots had already figured out: We had a malfunction and needed to return to Lima.

What a letdown! As we were descending toward Lima, I was hoping that the evaluation team would give us another chance to show them the airplane after we replaced the wastegate controllers. We landed back in Lima without further problems. Five of the pilots were willing to go for another demonstration flight if we could do it within seven days. The major reluctantly agreed as well.

As soon as we parked the airplane, we got on the phone to Wichita. I talked to Gart and gave him a report of what had happened. I told him that if he could rush a couple of wastegate controllers to us, we might salvage the deal, but we only had one week. He said he would ship them immediately

It was Friday, April 2, and we figured (and hoped) that the parts would arrive on the following Monday. I would install the controllers on Tuesday, test fly the airplane on Wednesday, and go for the demonstration flight on Thursday. According to the deadline the evaluation team had given us, we actually had until Friday.

During the weekend, as Ralph and I waited for the parts to be delivered, we enjoyed some sightseeing in Lima, the hotel amenities, and even had dinner at the house of the U.S. Consul General in Lima. Little did we know what disappointment was ahead.

Not only was the package not there on Monday morning, but it also still had not arrived by Tuesday. Gart couldn't believe it! After tracing the parts shipment, he was told that, for some unexplainable reason, the parts had gone to London, England, instead of Lima, Peru. They were being returned to Wichita; in the meantime, he was shipping another set of wastegate controllers to us, but they probably wouldn't get to Lima until that Friday. It didn't bode well. It would simply not be enough time. To make matters worse, the Peruvian Air Force told us that we had to move up the demonstration to that Thursday because the final decision had to be made on Friday.

The parts finally arrived Friday at noon. I installed the new wastegate controllers, but it was already too late. Just as I was shutting down the engines, I saw Ralph walking toward the airplane, giving me the "cut" signal. The deal was dead. When he entered the cabin, he told me that the Peruvian Air Force had already signed the deal with another company. We experienced the agony of defeat.

New Territory

We finished out our South American trip and flew back to Wichita in an airliner. It wasn't the triumphal return we wanted, but we did have eight firm orders and ten deposits for possible purchases within six months, which wasn't too shabby.

As soon as I debriefed Gart on the Peruvian Air Force fiasco, I began preparations to move to San Francisco and start operations from the new Western region offices. The logistics for the operation were staggering, and on top of all that, we had to fly six airplanes to San Carlos Airport near San Francisco.

On Monday, May 10, 1965, I loaded my family into a Cessna 206, with enough clothes to last us two weeks, for our new home in San Francisco. We found a very nice home the following day. It was on the top of the hills that divide the Pacific Ocean from the San Francisco Bay, with a view of both. We had settled into our new home and furnished the office by the end of May. Tony and I flew to Wichita to bring the last two airplanes to San Carlos Airport.

Serving Difficult People

I continued working with the distributors, dealers, and customers in my territory, finally gaining their confidence. I found it particularly difficult to work with one distributor. It took an extraordinary situation to reverse my relationship with him. I was visiting the distributor at Long Beach, California, when I received a call from Jim Wood, the distributor in Phoenix.

One of his best customers had called and told him that they had to make an emergency landing in Coalinga, California, and needed a new engine. He needed to be in Amarillo, Texas, two days later.

"What is Cessna going to do about it?" he asked me.

Our relationship had been strained ever since I started serving the entire Western region. Jim's perception of Cessna's personnel was that all we were interested in was getting him to buy more airplanes and parts, and that we wouldn't do much to provide service to him as a distributor, or his dealers and customers. I saw this as an opportunity to change Jim's erroneous perception with exceptional service.

I told him to call his customer and tell him I would be arriving at Coalinga in two hours and that he could use my demonstrator, a twin-engine 310, to fly to Amarillo. We would install a new engine on his airplane and deliver it to Amarillo within three days.

He was dubious because he had already called Continental to get a new engine and they were closed for the next five days, but I told him I would be there with a new engine waiting for them the next afternoon.

I hung up the phone and called Gart at the factory. I briefed him on what was going on and told him how important it was to get a new engine to Coalinga by the next day.

"This is a very short notice, but I'll see that you get that engine," he said.

I was airborne thirty minutes later, on my way to Coalinga. During the hour and ten minutes that it took me to fly to my destination, I began to wonder if I had overreacted in promising Jim that I would take care of the problem that quickly.

When I arrived in Fresno and assured the customer that I was from Cessna and was there to help, she and her pilot seemed relieved. I told them my demonstrator was at their disposal, and that a new engine would be installed on their 411 and would be delivered wherever they wanted it. She said she wanted it delivered to Amarillo's Tradewind Airport.

As soon as we preflighted the plane, gassed it up, and filed a flight plan, they were happily on their way. I waved good-bye to them as they were taxiing out. I was glad everything turned out the way it did. The first phase of my promise had been completed. Now I had to go to work on phase two: getting a Continental engine within twenty-four hours. And it was the Friday beginning the three-day Memorial Day weekend.

When I called the main office, I was pleasantly surprised that, by some miracle, Gart had been able to secure an engine from Cessna's military division, and he asked me where I wanted it shipped. What a relief! I told Gart to have it shipped to the Cessna dealer at Fresno Yosemite International Airport.

I called Jim Wood in Phoenix to confirm that two mechanics were being sent by Saturday morning. He said that they were booked on a flight to Fresno in two hours, so they would be arriving at the airport Friday at 1830. He then asked me if I had an engine.

"Of course! Didn't I tell you I would?"

He couldn't believe it.

"Hey, that's what regional service managers do," I told him. I laughed, and for the first time since I met Jim, I heard him laugh too. Outstanding service had finally won him over.

The mechanics and I worked hard to get the new engine installed and off to Jim in Phoenix by March 30. As we taxied in and he was approaching the airplane, I could see a smile on his face.

"I didn't think you could do it," he said as he shook my hand. Then he said, "Do you know what? If you ever decide to leave Cessna, you can have any job you want in my organization. I mean it!"

The plane would still need a couple of days to be fully functional again, but the client was happy and Jim was happy, and that was all that mattered. It was one of the most rewarding experiences in my life. I had spent a lot of time worrying about my relationship with this distributor, but I knew that things would now be different.

I thanked Jim for his offer and told him I would keep it in mind, and that for the time being all I wanted was the opportunity to work with him in my performance as a Cessna representative. When you live your life with service, you put the needs of others before your own and do whatever it takes to maintain your integrity in your work, home, and relationships. In doing so, you often find that you are rewarded one hundredfold. I know that some of my most fulfilling moments were those when I was serving others. *Live your life with service!*

Questions

1. The author started his journey with Cessna perfectly qualified for the regional service manager position with his hours of flying experience, mechanical background, and ability to speak Spanish. It was almost as if the position were designed for him. Do you believe in destiny or a divine plan for your life?

2. The author loved the challenges of his new position and working with others to serve them as customers, distributors, and dealerships. Do you see your current job or field as an opportunity to serve?

3. The author faced a major disappointment in Lima when his demonstration with the Peruvian Air Force did not go as planned, and he lost out on a big sale despite doing everything he could. What can you do when you are faced with situations that are out of your control?

4. When dealing with a distributor that did not trust him yet, the author went out of his way to provide exceptional customer service to win him over. When you are dealing with difficult people, are you more apt to retaliate with a bad attitude or to win them over with kindness? Explain.

Life Lesson #16

Live Your Life with APPRECIATION

"As we express our gratitude, we must never forget that the highest appreciation is not to utter words, but to live by them."

—John F. Kennedy Jr.

I continued servicing my territory with Cessna, enjoying every challenge and opportunity that came my way. I was a firm believer in the saying, "There are no problems, only unsolved opportunities." And I had plenty of those!

I was so involved with the needs of the distributors, dealers, and customers that I didn't have time to look after my own personal situation. It wasn't until one payday, after I paid all my bills, that I realized I was completely out of money, and I only got paid once a month. This situation had developed gradually, mainly because the living expenses were so much higher in San Francisco than they were in Wichita, and the adjustment I received in pay because of the move just wasn't enough. Of course, ultimately I should have spent more time managing our budget.

Just about the time I realized that we were in serious financial trouble, I read in an aviation magazine that United Airlines was hiring ground and flight personnel. It was the first time in many years that United was expanding. I visited the United Airlines employment office in San Francisco in the hopes of finding something in the field I desired.

This might be the opportunity I have been waiting for my whole life.

When I stepped into the employment office, there was a long line of men and women. My first reaction was to turn around and leave. I had a lot of work to do, and I didn't think I had the time to wait my turn. But then I thought, *Well, I'm here now, and maybe it won't take too long.*

After waiting in line for what seemed like an eternity, and considering leaving more than once, I was finally able to ask one of the attendants if United was hiring flight officers. When asked about my qualifications, I told her I had flown fighters and bombers in the Air Force, and that I was working for Cessna Aircraft Company at the present time. After asking my age, she said, "Please, come with me," and opened a door next to her window. *So far, so good.*

We went down a corridor to another door. She knocked and opened the door. She introduced me to Mr. Johnston and told him I was applying for a position as a flight officer. Mr. Johnston wanted to know what my qualifications were, and when I told him, he said, "When can you start?"

Wow!

I had been trying for ten years to fly for an airline with nothing but negative results and now I was being asked, "When can you start?"

"I would have to give Cessna at least two weeks' notice, and probably it would be more like a month before I could indoctrinate my replacement," I told him.

He encouraged me to not waste too much time due to the importance of the pilot seniority list and asked if he could call Cessna for references. I asked him to please wait until I had a chance to speak with my boss.

The whole situation was surreal, but I got back to my office late and had a million things to do. Finally I had time to call Gart in Wichita. Fortunately, he was still in the office. I told him I had just been offered a job flying for United Airlines, and I thought I would take it.

Gart didn't want me to be too hasty about my decision and offered me a position with Cessna that would provide more than enough income. I had mixed emotions about the two offers. On the one hand, I always wanted to fly for an airline. I finally had my opportunity, although being thirty-five years old and low on the pilot seniority list meant that I would be junior throughout my career. I would always get the most undesirable schedules, and I would always be at the tail end of assignments to move up from flight engineer to co-pilot, and from co-pilot to captain.

On the other hand, the offer from Cessna was very attractive, and I wouldn't have to go through the one-year probation at United, where the pay was minimal. It also sounded like a challenging and interesting position. In the final analysis, I had been bitten by the "bug" of flying for an airline my whole life, so I called Mr. Johnston and told him to initiate my application as a flight officer for United.

"Good choice and welcome aboard," he said. He told me to go to the flight office at San Francisco International Airport for an interview with the flight manager and that I would need to attend training classes.

I called Gart and told him I had accepted the offer from United, and that I was giving him my two-week notice. I shared how much I had enjoyed working under him, and how much I appreciated all his support during some of the difficult decisions I had to make as a regional service manager. Gart told me I was passing up a wonderful opportunity, but he wished me well in my new venture.

I finalized the transition with the new service manager and closed the door on that very enjoyable time in my life when I was able to fly an excellent fleet of airplanes, and serve some of the most outstanding people in the aviation world. I will always have a soft spot in my heart for the Cessna Aircraft Company, its dealer organization, and its customers.

A New Challenge

I called Mr. Johnston and told him I was ready to continue the hiring process at United Air Lines. I signed all the necessary forms, scheduled a physical examination, planned an interview with the flight manager the next day, and made plans to attend the first training class available at the training center in Denver, Colorado, which was the following Monday.

The flight manager wanted to know what kind of flying I had done, and the airplanes I had flown. I gave him a basic rundown of my experience, and he asked to see my logbooks and my flying license.

He reiterated what the hiring manager had told me that it was unlikely that I would ever make captain because of my age. But he encouraged me that even if I didn't get to fly as captain, it was still a very good job, the working conditions were great, and I would be guaranteed an excellent salary and a very good retirement.

"Who knows; if the airline industry grows as much as some experts think, even people in your age bracket and seniority status could make it to the left seat," he also told me.

As always, my optimism made me think that the airline industry would indeed grow beyond the present needs, and that I would eventually make it to the coveted left seat.

In Denver, the other thirty new hires and I had a two-hour indoctrination lecture where we were given our seniority list. According to the list, I was number 4,530 in the entire company. We started our second officer training, which consisted of one month of learning the DC-6 systems, one month of co-pilot training in the DC-6, and one month of learning company and FAA regulations, along with learning the duties of a second officer or flight engineer. At the end of the three-month training, we would have to pass an eight-hour oral examination by the Federal Aviation Administration. It was rumored that during that oral examination we had to have enough knowledge about the DC-6 to be able to tell the FAA inspector how to disassemble every system in the airplane and put it back together again. It was time to hit the books!

Our instructor started throwing all kinds of facts and figures at us about the DC-6, and there were more diagrams and schematics than I had ever seen in my years as a mechanic in the Air Force. Nevertheless, I had to learn it if I wanted to pass that nightmarish oral examination at the end of the course. Somehow I made it through the first day.

We began our basic flight officer training routine the next day. The studying of the DC-6 systems got really involved, and as motivated as I was to become a pilot for United, my heart just wasn't into learning what I considered to be an obsolete airplane, even though it had been a great airplane. As I was studying the hydraulic system, I noticed that there were two 727 openings available. I didn't know how the seniority system worked yet, but I thought that since I was the number two man in my class (because of my age), I should be able to get one of those 727 openings. I was right! The other student senior to me had the first choice of domiciles—one assignment was in New York and the other in Los Angeles. Since he was single, he didn't mind the idea of living in New York.

"You can have Los Angeles," he told me with a smile.

Talk about everything falling into place.

I thanked him profusely and shifted gears from learning all about the DC-6 to learning all about the Boeing 727 jetliner. I had a lot of enthusiasm when I started the 727 program because it was one of the newest jetliners, and I knew I was going to be flying out of Los Angeles. The days went by with busy schedules and a lot of anticipation for what was waiting for me right after training.

I was so close to my dream!

I finished the systems in the 727 and started introduction to first officer training. That was the most fun of the whole three months. I actually flew the airplane and demonstrated my ability shooting approaches and doing air work and a lot of simulator work.

The last month was the hardest. It was hours and hours of learning regulations, from airline regulations to FAA regulations. There were several two-inch thick books with small print for all the FAA regulations. There was also the flight operations manual (FOM) for the airline regulations. I spent all day studying, including during meals, and into the middle of the night. Suffice it to say that I had regulations coming out of my ears.

I had been converted into a potential Boeing 727 second officer by mid-June 1966. All I had to do was to prove it to the FAA, which would not be easy. You either know the airplane you are being assigned to, or you don't. I knew that, at the end of the day, I would either have a job, or I wouldn't. I had taken enough examinations to know when I was sufficiently prepared, so I shouldn't have been apprehensive about this one, but I was.

The Final Test

I would always remember the date of this exam, June 27, 1966, as I was missing Rhonda's fourth birthday. I found myself in one of the cubicles designated for oral examinations, with pictures of the 727 instrument panel and the flight engineer's panel on the wall, and a small table with two chairs. I sat at one of the chairs and started reviewing my knowledge of the 727 systems. When the

FAA inspector walked in, he introduced himself and started asking questions. We spent all day with the examination; by 1600 hours, he told me I had passed and walked out.

What a relief!

Things were looking great. We were measured for our uniforms, and I picked mine up at the same time I got my United Airlines diploma showing that I was a flight officer. I was given two weeks to report to my flight manager in Los Angeles. I flew back to San Francisco, rented a U-Haul truck, loaded my family in our car, and took off. Yolanda was seven years old, and Rhonda was four. We drove to Los Angeles during the Fourth of July weekend in 1966.

By the time we got settled in our new home, it was time for me to report to my flight manager at Los Angeles International Airport. His assistant welcomed me to the flight office and assigned me to my first trip on the line, which was scheduled for two days later.

It was an exhilarating moment, knowing that I had finally achieved what I had wanted to do since I was a young, starving fourteen-year-old boy in Mexico.

Appreciation for Living the Dream

It was finally time for my first flight!

My first flight as a flight engineer was going to be to Omaha, Nebraska, then continuing to New York City. The flight engineer supervisor would go with me to give me a check ride, since it was also my first flight as a second officer.

On Tuesday, July 5, 1966, I proudly donned the United Airlines uniform for the first time to fly out of Los Angeles International Airport, as the second officer on flight number 1755 bound for New York. I had spent the previous two days reviewing all of the second officer's duties, FAA regulations, company regulations, performance charts, and sharpening my knowledge of all the aircraft systems. I felt very confident when I walked into the dispatch office and met the captain and first officer with whom I was going to work the next three days.

I told them that it was my first trip, and that the flight engineer supervisor was going to be looking over my shoulder. The captain gave me a copy of the flight plan, the number of passengers, the weight and balance form, and the amount of fuel he had requested. One of my duties was to see that the requested amount of fuel was indeed loaded. The flight engineer supervisor and I checked all the fluid levels, the tires, landing gear mechanism, all the flight controls, and overall condition of the fuselage, empennage, and wings.

By the time the passengers began to board, the captain, first officer, and I were seated at our stations doing the final preparations for the flight. The flight engineer supervisor was seated behind me in one of the two jump seats, making sure I was taking care of all my duties. He had to prompt me once in a while, but, overall, I thought I was doing a good job. During the debriefing later that day, he went over all the phases of the two flights and gave me a few pointers on how to expedite my procedures.

Our layover hotel was the Plaza Hotel across the street from Central Park. It was my first visit to New York, and I enjoyed everything about it. I had plenty of time to go and explore the city. When I got back to my room, I reviewed all the information I had for the return trip to Los Angeles.

The flight back to Los Angeles was uneventful. By the time we landed, the flight engineer supervisor had already given me the certificate that allowed me to fly without supervision.

Everything seemed right with the world. I knew I had finally arrived at the first rung of the ladder that would eventually get me to the coveted "left seat" in the cockpit of a passenger airplane.

My next assigned trip was to New York via Chicago. I had reviewed the flight engineer procedures so much in my mind that I felt very comfortable flying this second trip. I was pleased with my performance during the flights from Los Angeles to New York and back, and I was happy that my career was settling into place. But there was to be much heartache in my home over the next year and a half.

Appreciation for Life

The part of my life that I wished could have been different had to do with Rhonda, my beautiful little girl. She was diagnosed with cancer when she was six and a half years old. Joyce and I could not believe this. We were sure the doctors would find a cure for our child. As the months progressed, Rhonda became worse and worse. I will never forget the caring and concern that management showed to my family at this time. They told me not to worry about my paycheck, but to take as long as I needed with my daughter.

Even as she worsened, and I needed more and more time with my family, United never changed their stance on my job. I took the time I needed, and the paychecks continued to arrive. We lost our dear daughter in February 1971, and our hearts were broken.

My gratitude to United can never be fully expressed. I would continue my entire career to give them the same kind of loyalty they showed to my family during our time of crisis.

Life After Loss

I decided to bid for a position as co-pilot in the 737s out of Chicago, since I did not want to fly as an engineer again. I got it!

That meant that I had to go back to Denver for training on the 737 and start planning to commute from Los Angeles to Chicago. I thought it would probably be about six months before I would be able to fly from Los Angeles again. I was wrong. I commuted from Los Angeles to Chicago for six long years.

I knew that Yolanda needed her father more than ever, now that she was an only child, and that made me very committed to family life when I was home. We enjoyed going to church together, playing tennis, riding bikes, and just chatting at length whenever Yolanda felt like it. I would stop whatever I was doing around the house when she wanted my attention.

Commuting was hard on the family and tedious for me, but flying the 737 was nothing but fun. It was as close to flying a fighter airplane as you could get while being a passenger airliner, because of its maneuverability in comparison to larger jets. As far as I was concerned, I was never overworked or underpaid, and I loved every minute I was in the air. The combination of flying the best-maintained airplanes and being proficient in all kinds of weather made our profession most satisfying.

It was sad that many pilots had forgotten the thrill of climbing into the atmosphere, the sound of rushing air, the growling of the powerful engines, the feeling of being one with the wind and one with the dark sky and the stars ahead. I kept myself from being dragged down by negative thinking because I was too busy enjoying the never-ending thrill of flying. I lived my life with appreciation because I had experienced both of the lowest points possible in life as well as the high ones. When you live with appreciation for all, even the small things in life, you are rewarded with a perspective that is always optimistic, no matter the circumstance. *Live your life with appreciation!*

Questions

1. The author left a great job with Cessna to pursue a career with United Airlines and fulfill his dream of becoming a passenger airline pilot. Do you agree with his decision? Why or why not?

2. Even though the United Airlines flight managers told the author that he would probably never make it to the captain's chair, he didn't give up hope and just appreciated the opportunity to be where he was. When your situation seems bleak and your dream seems unachievable, do you tend to give up? How can you use his example to keep pursuing your dream with passion?

3. The author had a deep appreciation for the opportunity to fly for United Airlines, even when he did not have the best assignments. He had a good attitude no matter where he was placed. Where in your life can you have a better attitude?

4. The author talks about how the other pilots had lost the thrill of flying and being part of the amazing miracle of aviation. We can do the same thing in our lives. What simple things can we look at more closely and thankfully in order to live with more appreciation?

Life Lesson #17

Live Your Life with DECISIVENESS

"Once you make a decision, the universe conspires to make it happen."

—Ralph Waldo Emerson

After about six or seven months in Chicago, I found out that it was going to take a lot longer to get back to the West Coast, if I wanted to do that. I had even considered moving to Illinois, but that was not one of the places where my family and I wanted to settle down. I continued commuting and tried to make all the extra travel time worthwhile. I would carry a briefcase containing all the paperwork, bills, and other items that I needed to handle, so I could use the limited time I had with my family to spend quality time with them.

After enjoying the 737 for six years, I realized I needed to make an effort to get back to California or once again consider moving to Illinois. Although I didn't expect to win an open bid for co-pilot on the DC-8 out of Los Angeles when it came up, I threw my name into the system just in case. To my surprise, when the bids came out, there I was, co-pilot for the DC-8 out of Los Angeles. I was elated about the transfer, although I was not thrilled about the plane.

I was given some of the worst routes, since I was very junior in my seniority for the DC-8. These routes included cargo liner overnight flights, starting at eleven or twelve at night. I would fly all night, spend the day at my destination, and then fly back the following night. It really wasn't so bad. I am a night owl by nature,

163

and these flights were just up my alley. I loved the opportunity to enjoy the stars and the moon as I flew each night, and I also received extra pay, which was always much appreciated.

Tough Decisions

I wish things had been as smooth on the home front as my landings had become. With the pain of losing our child, and then my being away so much with the many years of commuting, Joyce and I had become estranged from one another. Instead of the husband and wife we had once been, we seemed more like polite guests when we were together in our home. I felt a strong sense of duty as a parent to the one child we still had. Now that Yolanda was off to college, I knew I had to give both Joyce and myself the freedom we needed. After a serious discussion one day after work, we agreed to a divorce. My heart and my finances took a hit as a result of our divorce, but I still believe that it was the right thing to do, so we could both continue to grow and love as individuals.

Deciding to Try Something New

One day I received a letter in the mail inviting any pilots who would like to be considered for instructor positions to write a handwritten letter to the company expressing their interest. The pay would be comparable to what was paid to captains flying the 737s, which was double what I was currently earning. After the divorce, I was feeling the burden of the heavy financial responsibility, so this pay raise seemed like an answer to prayer. I got busy writing my letter to United.

I was chosen to come to the training center and show them what I knew. After a series of tests to show my knowledge and skills when it came to flying, I was to finish with a verbal interview with the vice president in charge of training. He congratulated me and mentioned that I was very well qualified and that he would look forward to having me as an instructor there.

When he asked me why United should consider me for the position, I got cold feet; I didn't want to be one of the feared check airmen on the annual check rides. I made a dumb, split-second decision and answered that I thought the other applicants were more qualified. I knew that I would regret those words once I said them, but I have always told myself that when you have made a decision, you stick with it.

Fortunately, I ended up with a second chance. I got a letter in the mail a few months later stating that I should call them immediately if I was still interested in the position of instructor in Denver. This time there was no reluctance on my part, and I made the right decision. In no time I had signed a contract and was told the company would sell my house for me and take care of my moving expenses.

"You are now part of management," I was told.

Welcome aboard.

At the same time that relief flooded through me, I began to wonder if I would have what it took to be a good instructor. *What if I am not up to the challenge?* But I had made the decision to do this, and I would go into it like everything I started—with determination and a good attitude.

I had an enjoyable drive to Denver, and I began training as soon as I arrived. They assigned me an instructor, Tom Savage, to teach me the art of teaching. I had been his student at one time and I knew he was an excellent instructor.

"If you are doing this for the money, just forget it," was the first thing Tom told me and the other trainees. "But if you learn to love this work, like I do, then you will be able to instruct. Without the love of the work, it will be impossible to be a good instructor."

I finished the training and was given my first class to instruct. It was time to pass on what I had learned! I enjoyed the classroom and simulator teaching, but I was a little hesitant with my first class. I came well prepared, however, and the students seemed to respond well to my teaching. I became more and more confident as an instructor, and at times would give extra help to pilots who were struggling with specific flying challenges, most of whom just needed an extra dose of confidence.

I had been instructing for about six months when all the instructors were notified that we should prepare ourselves to be promoted to the position of captain. In order to qualify, an applicant had to have a minimum of one thousand five hundred hours of flying time, pass a first class physical examination, and pass the Airline Transport Pilot (ATP) test, which is the equivalent of a PhD in other professions. And, of course, the applicant had to pass the most rigorous flying test of his career.

I met all the requirements: I had more than nine thousand hours of flying time, I had been taking the first class physical examination every six months, and I had taken the ATP test a couple of years before my assignment to the training center. The only reason I wasn't a captain yet was because I didn't have the seniority to bid for the captain position even in the most junior airplane. So this was one of the perks of being an instructor and a check airman.

I was assigned to take my check ride in the simulator and in the airplane with an FAA inspector. The simulator check took place January 7, 1983. It was reminiscent of my check ride when I finished the Air Force pilot training in 1958. Then, a few days later, I successfully completed the check ride in the airplane and was signed off as a 727 captain. From then on, I felt like I was living my dream every single day.

I continued with the busy training schedule, gaining more confidence in my instructing ability. I spent hours preparing to give the students the most realistic flying simulation I could, with weather conditions, temperature, altitude, mechanical failures, and even incorporated the peculiarities of any airport in the world.

The students gained the proficiency required of an airline pilot in a fraction of the time and cost of going through similar training in an actual airplane. By the time they finished the simulator portion of their training, they were ready to fly the airplane in their position, either as first officer or captain, anywhere in the world. When the students finished the simulator portion of the training, they flew a number of hours with a check pilot in the airplane.

Within a few months, my manager was moved up to the 747. He wanted to take his best instructors with him, and so I began training pilots on the 747. This meant that I would now be a captain on the 747, which was the largest plane in our fleet. I would need to fly the line at least once every other month so I would be proficient in training. I would just displace a captain on whatever route I wanted, which was a win-win since he still got paid for the flight.

Handling Bad Decisions

While I was in the middle of all this training and flying, I made a rather dumb investment and lost a lot of money. I decided I needed some good advice before making any other monetary decisions, so I attended a financial seminar by an advisor named Ellen Olsen. It was interesting, but a lot of it went over my head. However, Ellen wanted to help, and she had me fill out a survey that asked questions about my financial knowledge and situation.

After a couple of weeks, she asked me to come to the office to review my financial needs. I kept seeing her now and then, on a business level. I must say, though, that this fifty-two-year-old lady with a winning smile and beautiful face had caught my attention on a personal level as well.

She assisted me by going above and beyond when I couldn't be home to pay some bills that were due. This was before automatic payments and the Internet, so I had to rely on her good nature to help me out. At the time, my mother had come from Mexico to live with me. Ellen not only took care of my bills, but also took my mother to lunch. Ellen had become fluent in Spanish when she lived in Guadalajara, Mexico, some years previously, and my mother was delighted to have someone to visit with in her native tongue.

When I returned from Chicago, I wanted to thank Ellen for her generous help, so I invited her to dinner at a restaurant at the airport called the 94th Squadron. There were big picture windows where you could sit and watch the planes taking off and landing. They also had headsets at the tables so you could hear the conversations between the pilots and air traffic control. We had a wonderful time as we ate and watched the sun setting.

That was the beginning of our friendship. We continued to see one another and our relationship grew stronger and stronger. I really had no intention of ever marrying again, but she said she knew I was the man for her almost immediately. We continued seeing each another and completely enjoyed each other's company. One day it came to the point where it was clear that Ellen wanted to marry, but I still did not feel that way. So she told me it would probably be better if we did not see each other anymore.

I didn't realize how much, as the song goes, "I had grown accustomed to her face." I couldn't even last one day. I called her the next day.

"Listen, Ellen, I was wrong," I said. "I really love being with you. We can get married, if that is what you want." I felt like the right decision was to keep her in my life, whatever that meant. She didn't want me to feel like she had pressured me into marriage, so she said we could continue on as we had been doing, enjoying each other's company and growing in love.

It was a short time later that we were married. It was one of the best decisions I have ever made.

When you live your life with decisiveness, you will be faced with the possibility of both failure and success as a result of those decisions. I knew that my decision to turn down the instructor position was one I'd regret, but I was fortunate enough to get a second chance. I made the decision to give marriage and love another chance with Ellen, and I have been continually blessed by that decision. You have to have the courage to take decisive action and keep moving forward to your dream. *Live your life with decisiveness!*

Questions

1. The author made the tough decision to stop commuting back and forth to Chicago and find whatever employment he could with United out of Los Angeles. He was thrilled to be able to fly a DC-8, even though it meant flying at night. Being close to his family was his most important motivating decision. How do others affect your decision-making process? Give examples.

2. After initially declining the position of instructor, the author made the decision to teach when given a second chance. In addition to the increase in pay, he received the opportunity to pass on all that he had learned in his flight experience. Why is it so rewarding to teach others what you know?

3. After facing some financial trouble, the author sought help with a local financial advisor. It turned out to be a good decision on two levels since she both helped him get his finances in shape and also became a very good friend. What good decisions have you made in the past that turned into something more than you expected?

Life Lesson #18

Live Your Life with PURPOSE

"The purpose of life is a life of purpose."

—Robert Byrne

Ellen would remind me every once in a while that retirement was coming up, and I should be doing everything I needed to prepare. In my own mind I could not imagine quitting. Flying was my life. I was at my peak professionally and in perfect health, so I could not understand the retirement requirement regulations.

But like everything else in life, the dreaded retirement day arrived.

This date happened to coincide with my mother's death. She passed away on July 5, 1991. My final flight would be on my birthday, July 14, 1991. For a pilot's final flight, it is customary to let the captain have all of the landings for that day. I landed in Chicago, had an eight-hour layover, and then took the plane back to San Francisco. I landed the plane, taxied to the gate, shut down the engines, and that was it.

One day I could fly, and the next day I couldn't. I felt like I had lost my purpose in life.

This chapter in my life came to an end, and I was just not ready. I had to face the facts and realize my days of flying for United Airlines were over.

A New Purpose

Now what was I going to do? One day while I was reading *Flying* magazine, I came across an article about the Experimental Aircraft Association (EAA) that promoted the building of your own airplanes. In the early years, people would build a plane from the ground up, figuring out their own materials every step of the way. Several factories around the United States made kits for a variety of airplanes. As I began my research on what was available, I thought, *This is an attractive alternative to get me in the air again, but I really don't know anything about building from a kit.* Sure, I had worked as an airplane mechanic in the Air Force, but building an entire plane was a whole other matter.

I started looking around for kits that were available in my area and considered where I would conduct a project of this size. I looked into the cost of buying a hangar, which led me to Front Range Airport. It was about a forty-five minute drive from my house, but I could see there were people actually building planes in their hangars.

In one of these hangars, I met a young man by the name of Charles Brenner, or Chuck, as he was called. He was busy working on a plane, and you could tell he was passionate about what he was building. He was an artist in his field, and I liked him right away. He had a great attitude when I told him I was thinking of building a plane.

"Well, building planes is my passion. In fact, I have a kit that I won't be able to get to. It is right over there," he said, pointing to a corner of the hangar. "If you want to buy that Lancair 360 two-seater kit, I will help you build it."

I liked the idea of having a building partner, and the price for the kit was reasonable. So I went home to think about it. I knew I had the time and the interest. I decided it would be another good phase for my life. I went back to the airport to let Chuck know I was in.

It was only twenty-five thousand dollars for the kit, but I could already see that this project would eventually become a money pit, as each item not included was very expensive. We agreed that Chuck would show me what to do, and then I would do the work. We got started the very next week.

I remember opening the boxes and taking out the instruction manuals, which were each about two inches thick. It was a bit overwhelming. Typically, builders could take up to five years to build a plane, but I was determined to have my plane done in one year. I figured I was getting old, so I felt like I needed to finish my plane while I still had time to be a pilot.

Chuck felt like finishing in one year was a very ambitious goal, and it would require a couple more guys helping since he was already committed to several projects. We hired Phil Bowman, an airplane mechanic at Front Range Airport, and Dave Vogel, a genius when it came to electronics. I wanted to work every single day because I was serious about finishing in one year. I'd be out there doing whatever I could, installing the controls, and setting up the engine mounts.

When I was ready for the engine, I chose one from Lycoming with one hundred eighty horsepower. I remembered looking at that brand-new engine. It was beautiful! I had already purchased the propeller that was six thousand dollars. The engine was twenty-three thousand, the instrument panel was fifteen thousand, and the radios were about five thousand. I had estimated my project would cost me about seventy-five thousand dollars. In reality it would end up costing me over one hundred fifty thousand dollars. I was right, indeed, about that money pit idea.

Consequently, I ran out of money. I took out a loan on my house. I hated to do that because I had just paid it off. However, I was determined to see this project completed. And, sure enough, almost to the day one year later, it was time to get the plane ready for flight. But I was in for another speed bump.

We were getting ready to put fuel in the tanks, and I decided to scrutinize them carefully, mostly out of curiosity. I put my flashlight into the wings for a good view, and what I saw made my heart sink. The sealing material that keeps the fuel from leaking out was blistering away from the interior of the skin. It had not cured properly, and the wings would not be able to hold fuel. It was a disaster! I found out that the parts department had sent us the wrong materials.

I went home thinking about just scrapping the whole project, selling off the parts, and donating the plane to a training school. When I told Ellen the whole story, including my desire to give up, she said, "Oh no! You can't stop now. There must be a way to fix the problem."

I explained to her why nothing would work, but she persisted.

"You must think of something, Don," she said. "It would be a shame to see all of your hard work go for nothing."

I was driving to the airport a few days later, my mind full of dark thoughts. I usually have the radio on, but I was in no mood for listening to music. My usual optimism was nowhere to be found. I planned to just stew the whole forty-five minute drive to the airport. I had convinced myself that the best plan was to sell the plane and just forget it. Since I figured I had solved my dilemma, I turned the radio on just before I got to the airport.

Just as I turned it on, the announcer said, "And now, 'The Impossible Dream,' by Robert Goulet." After the song ended, I thought, *How can I quit after hearing 'The Impossible Dream'?* So I started calling my project "The Impossible Dream."

My purpose was renewed. I decided I was going to fix it no matter what it took.

Restoring the Impossible Dream

I had to actually cut the skins off of the wings to cut the panels from the bottom of the wings. I was careful to miss the ribs. I also had to painstakingly scrape off all the bad compound from the remaining parts. People saw me doing this and thought I'd gone crazy.

The company that sent the wrong materials made it right by sending me two new wing panels as well as the right materials for the sealant. I carefully applied the new sealant and made sure every detail was correct this time. All of this work took an additional year to complete. Finally, on October 30, 1995, my plane was ready to be airborne.

I made a quick flight on a similar airplane to become oriented with its flight systems. When I was ready to fly my own plane, Chuck got the video camera and positioned himself at the end of the runway for a good view for recording. I gave my plane a fast taxi test on the runway and everything felt good, so I taxied back.

I added power, accelerated to takeoff speed, barely pulled back on the control stick, and the plane took off like a homesick angel. I went around the pattern and finished my short test flight, while Chuck recorded my historic flight.

It was a great plane that flew like a little fighter. I barely moved the stick and the plane responded. It looked ugly, because we had not painted it yet, but to me it was beautiful. I felt that I had accomplished another great feat. I did dream the "Impossible Dream," and I made it come true. Even though I had to endure the financial strain of such a large undertaking and all of the disappointments along the way, putting myself into building that airplane gave me purpose. It was something I so desperately needed after retiring from United Airlines and suddenly finding myself without direction. Whatever your purpose is in life, pursue it with a passion. Don't let obstacles or disappointments stop you from realizing it. Fulfill your "Impossible Dream," just as I achieved mine. *Live your life with purpose!*

Questions

1. Upon retiring from United Airlines, the author found himself without a life purpose since he had fulfilled his dream of becoming an airline pilot. He felt unmoored and needed direction. Why is it so important for us to have purpose in our lives?

2. Building an airplane from the ground up proved to be the perfect challenge for the author when he was searching for purpose. But it came with a steep price tag with all of the expenses. How much is it worth to you to find your purpose? Would you invest as much as the author did? Why or why not?

3. Even when the author was disappointed by the bad materials he encountered in the wings that delayed his airplane project another year, he didn't give up. He called it his "Impossible Dream," after the Robert Goulet song. Do you have a dream that seems impossible and not worth the trouble? What if you "disassembled" it to find the flaws and started over?

4. If you don't know your life's purpose yet, begin to think about it. How can knowing your life purpose direct your everyday decisions and goals?

Life Lesson #19

Live Your Life with ADVENTURE

"Adventure is worthwhile in itself."

—Amelia Earhart

The Lancair gave me ten years of enjoyable flying. Its performance was unbelievable. It was so clean and aerodynamic. It could fly at two hundred thirty-five miles per hour with its one hundred eighty horsepower engine, almost twice the speed of other airplanes of the same size.

I had many memorable flights in "Jonathan," the name I gave my airplane in memory of *Jonathan Livingston Seagull*, the book written by Richard Bach, the famous author. His story is about following your heart, making your own rules, and knowing there is more to living than meets the eye. It certainly resonated with me and fueled me to continue dreaming in my own life.

My most memorable flight occurred in 2003, when the entire country was celebrating the one hundredth anniversary of the Wright brothers first flight. I had the opportunity to join the EAA celebration by flying in a race from Kitty Hawk, North Carolina, where the Wright brothers built their airplane, to Dayton, Ohio, which is where they lived. That was the first leg. Then we flew from Dayton to Oshkosh, Wisconsin, where EAA AirVenture is celebrated every year.

To prepare for that race, I had to apply and be approved. A limited number of participants were allowed in this event, and I had to tell them why I wanted to do it, what kind of airplane I had, and what the Lancair's speed would be for the race. I was elated when I got a letter saying I was accepted. I was given a number for my plane and told to be at Dare County Regional Airport, which is about ten miles south of Kitty Hawk, the day before the race.

After my short qualification flight, I radioed in and told them I was headed to visit Kitty Hawk. I had always wanted to see Kitty Hawk, because I had studied much about the Wright brothers and their importance in the history of aviation. I could just picture the whole adventure these brothers had as they were literally changing history.

And They're Off!

The next day it was time for the race. We took off in intervals of ten seconds. We flew first to Kitty Hawk, because that is where they would check our starting time. Then we headed for Dayton. I came down low enough for them to check my number, and then I was off. It was enjoyable to see airplanes all around me. Some of them would pass me, and then I would pass some of them. Airplanes were all over the sky.

The flight from Kitty Hawk to Dayton was exciting. My place was number nine out of eighty-four participants. Only one airplane didn't make it. My spirits were high as I neared Dayton International Airport; I was pleased with how green and immaculate it was kept in honor of the Wright brothers. All the planes that had landed prior to me were neatly parked at an angle in the grass, so I joined them and turned to enjoy the view of the rest of the racers coming in and landing.

We were supposed to leave the next morning to head to Oshkosh, but terrible weather sidelined us. We waited for the conditions to improve, but we weren't able to continue until the next day. About thirty-five minutes out of Dayton, we could see dark clouds and fog going all the way to the ground. Some guys took a chance and went right into the bad weather.

I chose to go above it, but I lost a lot of time by doing so, and I paid for that later. As we neared Aurora Air Park just west of Chicago, we had to descend to a lower altitude so the ground crew could see our airplane number and record our time. I was about one hundred feet off the ground, and I encountered the biggest swarm of gnats I have ever seen. They completely covered my windshield, and I could not see a thing.

We finally got to Lake Winnebago, which was actually part of the Oshkosh airport. I flew over the raft on the lake that was our final spot to have our times recorded, pulled my plane up, and I could see Wittman Regional Airport.

It was great to see Chuck Brenner waiting for me at Oshkosh, and he even helped me get my bug-covered windshield looking good again. The rest of the day was like a dream. All of the participating pilots were acknowledged with plaques showing their speed and time in the race, and we all enjoyed a scrumptious banquet. We stayed there that night and spent the next day looking at planes and enjoying the air shows. It was, without a doubt, my most memorable time with my Lancair.

As I was heading home, I landed in a little airport in Illinois to spend the night. They knew what I had been doing, and everyone wanted to see the airplane. It was a big deal to fellow flying enthusiasts.

I asked a man at the airport if any hangars were available; to my surprise, he offered the hangar to me at no cost. I was really given the royal treatment in that little town. I spent the night, and then headed home the next morning. I chalked this up to another dream come true.

The Beginning of yet Another Adventure

Shortly after my Kitty Hawk adventure, I decided to sell the Lancair. I had discovered that Chuck was interested in buying it. I looked around at the type of planes that were being bought and sold in 2007, and one in particular—a Cirrus four-seater with a supercharged engine—caught my eye. I called it a computer on wings, as everything was now done electronically. This also meant the price was very steep. I was able to join a group of three other men that wanted to buy this plane as a joint venture.

I wasn't completely comfortable with the electronic way of flying, but the thought of staying on the ground was more of a problem, in my mind, than learning a new flying system. All I had to do was program everything in—the rate of climb, the altitude, the heading, the speed, the route I wanted to fly—and that was it. I would just take off, engage the autopilot, cross my arms, and watch it do its stuff. And it made me sick, because it did it perfectly! I took a few flights where I would just disengage the autopilot, as I much preferred to be the pilot in charge. There was no question that it was an amazing airplane, but I just never got used to it.

My last flight in my Cirrus was to attend my Aviation Cadet Reunion in Dayton, Ohio, at the Wright Patterson Museum. It was great to see my old buddies from Aviation Cadet Class 59-A. We were treated to a banquet while an Air Force band played for our pleasure.

Unfortunately, I would end up having to sell my share of the plane. I lost half of what I called my "airplane account" when the stock market plunged. I could not keep up with the expenses due to high fuel prices and maintenance.

Questions

1. What is something that is on your "bucket list" to complete in your lifetime? Share your possible or already-completed adventure(s). What does the possibility of an adventure add to your life?

2. During the Kitty Hawk to Dayton race, in commemoration of the Wright brothers, the author was able to enjoy the experience of being around so many other airplane enthusiasts. How can being around like-minded people help you as you work to achieve your dream?

3. When he bought the highly technical Cirrus airplane, the author was frustrated by the systems that were unfamiliar to him. He preferred being in control of the plane. Can you identify with wanting to be in control? Are there areas of your life where you would benefit from delegating some control?

4. The author shares his uncertainty and dread as his career as a pilot finally comes to an end. Share a time that you were faced with an ending that you were not ready to experience.

Life Lesson #20

Live Your Life With a DREAM

"There is nothing like a dream to create the future."

—Victor Hugo

As the vibrations and comforting hums of the Cirrus engine faded, my mind slowly shed the cobwebs still clinging after sleep. I remembered that day, so long ago, when I was a young boy in Mexico and had vividly dreamed of flying.

After that dream, I had awakened slowly to the familiar morning sounds: my mother stirring in the kitchen, humming softly to herself as she made breakfast for my sister and me; my stepfather listening to the radio; a dog barking in the distance.

On that morning, I sat up and stretched, shaking off the last bit of slumber. Although I would be thirteen the following month, I didn't know if anything was planned or what I was imagining. But I had an expectation of something wonderful about to happen in my life. I suppose it was my mother's optimism that fueled my hope. She always told me that we may have been broke, *but we were rich in the things that mattered.*

My mother was a beautiful woman with an endless supply of optimism. No matter how bad things got—and they got very bad—her optimism was always there to see us through. She woke up happy and looked forward to each day. Life was a joy to her, and no one around her could be depressed.

One of my mother's favorite sayings was, "Yesterday is a canceled check; tomorrow is a promissory note; today is cash.

185

Use it!" She lived every day to the fullest and was never satisfied with the ordinary. There was no one like her.

I stretched once more, rubbed my eyes, and then shuffled in to help my mother with the huevos, tortillas, and other breakfast accompaniments. My dream from the previous night still shadowed me in the bright daylight of the kitchen. *Had I really just dreamed of becoming a pilot?* It all seemed so vivid and real that I could not shake the feeling that it was somehow a prediction for my future.

I reached out to greet and hug my mother, who was always delighted by my affections. I considered telling her about my dream, but I hesitated for a moment, not sure of how my imagination would be received.

Finally, I decided to share my story. My mother listened quietly as she deftly turned tortilla after tortilla in the cast iron skillet. When I finished, she seemed to be considering my dream with more credence than I dared to anticipate. She finally turned to me, and her eyes locked on mine.

"You are capable of anything you put your mind to," she said firmly. "If you want to be a pilot, I believe in you. Donald, you have the ability to be greater than you could ever possibly imagine. Don't ever forget that."

She unceremoniously handed me the eggs to prepare for our meal, and my heart warmed to her encouragement. I smiled as we worked together in the kitchen. She had always urged me to be an individual and to be a leader, not a follower. My mother always said that if there was anything I could do about a problem, I should do it. If not, I shouldn't worry about it.

"Whatever must happen, will happen," she would always say.

And happen it did. On that fateful morning, little did I know that we would soon endure unthinkable trials, as a result

186

of my stepfather leaving us. It was a true test of our belief that things would work out as they should. We barely survived the horrendous financial instability, and spent many nights in hunger, but our circumstances would never defeat us, thanks to my mother's untiring optimism.

Even when we had to sell all of our belongings, we had a hope for the future. A few weeks later, I set out walking to sell our most prized painting. As I fought a high wind that was threatening to tear the painting from my hands, I was tempted to think that we were reaching the bottom of a pit. *What was to become of us? What about my dream?*

However, when I returned with the money from selling the painting, my mother was her usual self: cheerful and already making plans to go on with our lives. She could have chosen to despair, think negatively, or even throw in the towel. But she did everything she could with the problem at hand, and she did it with an uncanny optimism for the future. I remember my mother standing in our apartment with our few remaining possessions, a smile on her face and astonishing hope for the future. We were going to make it.

Unfortunately, I now understood that my birthday would come and go again without fanfare, as it had many times in the past. I was disappointed, but I had been given a glimpse of what my life could become if I just persevered. I decided then and there that no matter what I faced in my life, I would keep my mother's optimism close, and I would hold on to my dream. Even though I would receive no birthday presents when I turned thirteen that year, I had already received the most precious of gifts—*the gift of a dream.*

I determined to believe that my dream was possible, and I knew that I would take small steps toward achieving it every day. I would NEVER give up. I imagined myself out in the wind again, but this time I leaned into the gale and held fast to my dream. Nothing could stop me.

I had seen in my dream what was possible, and I knew beyond a shadow of a doubt that I would create that future for myself—day by day, week by week, and year by year. It was in that very moment that my dreams took flight. I closed my eyes, stretched out my arms, and felt myself soaring above the clouds once again.

"It starts with a dream. Add faith, and it becomes belief.
Add action, and it becomes a part of life.
Add perseverance, and it becomes a goal in sight.
Add patience and time, and it becomes
a dream come true."

—Doe Zantamata

Live your life with a dream!

Questions

1. The author states that his family may have been broke, but they *were rich in the things that mattered*. What are some of the things in your life that are not monetary but add value to your life?

2. The author states that his mother's favorite saying was, "Yesterday is a canceled check; tomorrow is a promissory note; today is cash. Use it!" What does this saying mean to you?

3. The author's mother told him to be an individual and to be a leader, not a follower. What are some of the areas in your life where you need to be more of a leader?

4. Do you have a dream? If not, start thinking about the things that bring you joy and make you tick. If you do, are you actively pursuing it? Why or why not?

5. What steps can you take today, this week, or this month to make your dream a reality? Remember, you don't always have to take big steps. Little ones will move you in the right direction too.